BIRMINGHAM HERITAGE

Foreword by the Rt Hon Roy Jenkins
President of the European Commission

BIRMINGHAM HERITAGE

Joan Zuckerman and Geoffrey Eley

CROOM HELM   LONDON

© 1979 Joan Zuckerman and Geoffrey Eley
Croom Helm Ltd, 2-10 St John's Road, London SW11

British Library Cataloguing in Publication Data

Zuckerman, Joan
    The Birmingham heritage.
    1. Birmingham, Eng. — History
    I. Title   II. Eley, Geoffrey
    942.4'96   DA690.B6

ISBN 0-85664-875-2

Printed and bound in Great Britain

Contents

Illustrations

PICTURE CREDITS

The authors and publishers wish to thank the following for permission to reproduce copyright illustrations:

Birmingham Publicity Section: pages 22, 25, 29, 31, 37, 44, 47, 73, 98, 128, 138, 143, 156, 157, 169, 177, 178-9; Birmingham Museums and Art Gallery, 24, 45, 57, 97, 128, 132-33, 139, 147, 169; Victoria and Albert Museum, 57, 100, 113, 160; Radio Times-Hulton Picture Library, 47, 172; Cogent Elliott Advertising, 20; Cambridge University, 67; Birmingham Mint, 73; National Portrait Gallery, 78; Royal Society, 79; Hugh McKnight Photography, 84-5, 87, 91; Science Museum London, 60-1, 104; Terence Cuneo, 107; Illustrated London News, 161; Wayland Picture Library, 163; Mrs J.P. Harvey Loynes, 171; and Birmingham Post, 174.

The remaining published photographs belong to Joan Zuckerman.

To the Scientists, Engineers and skilled Craftsmen
who made Birmingham the Toyshop,
then the Workshop of the World

Foreword

The Rt. Hon. Roy Jenkins
President of the European Commission

Birmingham is the second city of Britain. It was not the
second city of the Empire, as Glasgow (with perhaps a little
undercounting of the inhabitants of Calcutta and Bombay)
used to describe itself, for the Empire had mostly gone
before Birmingham overtook Glasgow in population. Nor was
Birmingham the best-known English manufacturing town of
the nineteenth century. That distinction, I suppose, must
belong to Manchester, which was both the centre of our
largest single early export trade and a place the name of
which was rather loosely associated with the philosophy of
the Industrial Revolution. Yet Birmingham, although sometimes despised for a rather anonymous materialism by those
who do not know it, is in my view richer in the diversity of
its history, the disparate distinction of its leading citizens
(Matthew Boulton, Joseph Priestley, Joseph Chamberlain, to
name only three) and its innovating quality, both in industrial process and civic government, than any other British
provincial town.

I do not think that this judgement is affected by the fact that
I have had the rewarding experience of representing a part of
it in Parliament for 27 years. From the time, before the
beginning of those 27 years, when I first began to know
Birmingham well, I was always fascinated by its capacity to
change without losing its sense of the past. It has long been
something of a melting pot, with 'incomers', from the Dissenters of the eighteenth and early nineteenth centuries, through
the Welsh of the inter-war years, the Irish of the forties and
the West Indians and the Asians of the last decade, making up
a substantial part of the population. It has torn itself down
and built itself up again (not always wholly happily) and

13

changed not only its buildings but the pattern of its streets. But it has always retained a large part of its tradition and its history. That tradition and history were based on few natural advantages. It is, of course, almost the centre of England, which has given it a junction role in the canal, railway and motor ages. But to be almost central is a somewhat imprecise concept, and it has few other advantages of site. Birmingham has no grand bay or river around which to develop. It had no medieval cathedral around which to cluster. It is not even in a welcoming hollow, but rolls over the undulating ground of a slightly bleak plateau, and one without any natural resources of mineral wealth. Its development has always been a triumph of man over nature, and the fact that (as the authors tell us) it has on its upland ground more canals than Venice, now mostly hidden but still rather mysteriously there, is a remarkable testimony to this.

The changes during the period I represented the city were immense. When I made my first political forays in Birmingham it was still recognisably Joseph Chamberlain's town. There was the rather confined centre, dominated by the neo-classical Town Hall, the later and more ornate Council House and the two rather cavernous nineteenth-century railway stations. The old adjacent areas of small workshops, most notably the Jewellery Quarter, were still largely intact. Trams still ran from murky city terminals out through the 'streets of small houses [which] fitted the townscape, easily climbing up and down the hills in warm red brick' (an evocative phrase of the authors) to the greener and somewhat more spacious inter-war areas beyond. Now nearly all that is greatly changed. If Joseph Chamberlain were to arrive at New Street station today and try to find his way out to his old house at King's Heath I fear that he would feel a lost stranger. Yet after a while he might find a few familiar landmarks and vistas — the old Midland Hotel, churches, pubs, and the prospect across Cannon Hill Park to the unmistakable campanile and other central buildings of the now vastly expanded University which he did so much to implant in Edgbaston at the turn of the century.

In trying to reconcile the new Birmingham with the old he or anyone else would find this book of Lady Zuckerman and Dr Eley of immense value and interest. There have been a lot of books about Birmingham. Some have been historical, some topographical, some just illustrated guides. But I know of nothing which blends the history and the topography as does this. It uses the 'Birmingham heritage' to illuminate the city of today.

Roy Jenkins
August 1978

Acknowledgements

During my last three years in Birmingham (I left the city in 1965) I collected notes and pictures for this book. Eighteen months ago I met Geoffrey Eley, a professional writer whose childhood was spent in Birmingham. He shared my own feelings about the city and together we decided to revise and update my work for publication.

Throughout the preparation of *Birmingham Heritage* I was much helped and encouraged by many friends. My husband, as usual, started it off without at all realising where it would lead!

I am particularly grateful to Roy Jenkins who spurred me on and who has now added to his kindness by writing a Foreword. I would also like to acknowledge Lord Mountbatten's generosity in allowing me to use the picture 'The Forge' by Joseph Wright (Broadlands Collection) on the front of the jacket. Throughout the years Sir John Betjeman's enthusiasm has been a constant encouragement.

A number of friends have read my early drafts and offered helpful suggestions. In particular, I should like to mention Sir Charles Burman, Mr Stephen Lloyd, Mr C.H. Gibbs-Smith, Mr James Holland, Mr John English, Mrs John Armstrong and Lady Harrod. To Mr and Mrs Arthur Chamberlain, Sir Adrian Cadbury, Mr Michael Hope, Sir Eric Clayton and Mr Derek Cotton I am indebted for their interest and the loan of rare books.

Finally, together with my co-author Geoffrey Eley I owe thanks to a number of City of Birmingham experts for their kind comments and criticism, as well as their unfailing courtesy in answering our questions and supplying information.

We would particularly like to thank Councillor H.N. Scrimshaw and Mr R.D. Siddall for their valuable help and advice; Sir Robert Booth for his concern and interest; also the City Librarian, Mr B.H. Baumfield, Miss Dorothy McCulla (Head of the Local Studies Department) and Mr P. Ashley (City Press Officer) for the additional information they so willingly provided.

Joan Zuckerman

Introduction

Birmingham has grown over twelve or thirteen centuries from a small Anglo-Saxon settlement into one of the major industrial centres of modern Europe. Today it incorporates the ancient Royal town of Sutton Coldfield and is a Metropolitan District within the West Midlands Metropolitan County. 'Made in Birmingham' are familiar words at home and across the seas. The phrase epitomises the skills and products which have made it the hardware centre of the world. As a trading nation the United Kingdom relies heavily upon the city of Birmingham — its people and factories account for a quarter of the entire nation's exports.

It is a lively city, strong and traditionally independent in spirit. Much of its strength comes from the nature of its people — visitors frequently comment on their helpful and warm-hearted ways. Above all it is a city which *cares* for its people, whether born 'Brummagems' or not. Its local inhabitants are notoriously hard-working, with a long tradition of looking outwards on life and encouraging new crafts and new industries.

In this age of world population interchange, inter-continental travel and flourishing tourism, few cities can rival Birmingham's facilities and commercial importance. A notable instance of helpfulness is the manner in which adult coloured immigrants have, in the course of time, been absorbed into its life-style and the coloured children into its traditionally progressive schools (when there *are* arguments they are concerned not with racialism but rather with the relative merits of Birmingham City or Aston Villa football teams!).

2. &. 3. The Zuckermans' former Edgbaston home — a late Regency house on the Calthorpe Estate (on right of illustration, behind a chestnut tree). Today Edgbaston, home of the University of Birmingham and its attached Queen Elizabeth Hospital, is an important consultant medical centre. In complete contrast, and only a few minutes' walk away, were the Victorian industrial slums — since demolished in the city's postwar rehousing schemes.

Although for centuries Birmingham has been an ever-changing city, the years since the last war have seen the most extensive redevelopment and the most important civic progress. This is apparent in the city's new buildings, in transport, in education (today there are no nineteenth-century slum schools left in Birmingham) and in industrial prestige. In 1976, to its variety of impressive post-war buildings — including a £15 million shopping centre — Birmingham added the National Exhibition Centre, the largest and most modern exhibition site in Britain. To this 'shop window' for industry an ever-increasing number of visitors and exhibitors now come from all parts of the world. It is, above all, the place where she proclaims herself part of the European industrial scene.

Birmingham is proud of its large population of skilled workers who, over the centuries, have enabled a vast quantity and variety of metal goods to pour from its factories and the hundreds of small workshops so characteristic of the city. As early as the sixteenth century, possibly even before, the country's metal trades concentrated in Birmingham. Later on, a network of canals was built, providing vital transport links with other cities and with the country's ports. Factories and workshops multiplied and, with the coming of the railway in the middle of the nineteenth century, Birmingham was in big business. It is, indeed, true to say that without her contribution — chiefly from the metal industries — the his-

20

tory of the entire United Kingdom over the past 250 years would have been very different.

The city has rightly been called 'the cradle of invention'. Here men engraved their names on the history of the world — men such as Matthew Boulton and James Watt, who perfected the steam engine; William Murdoch, inventor of gas lighting; and James Keir, a man of profound chemical knowledge. The saga of Birmingham's science and resulting industrial expertise is the basis of this book (but not the *entire* story of this fascinating but sometimes much misunderstood city!). Today Birmingham is the home of such world-renowned industries as Leyland Motors, Tube Investments, the Dunlop Rubber Company, Cadbury-Schweppes, Joseph Lucas, GKN, Albright and Wilson, and IMI. The city is still the centre of brass and copper manufacture and within this single city as many as a thousand or more trades, big and small, carry on their business.

Whilst industry is Birmingham's life-blood it has an equally proud and distinguished record in science, the arts and in sport. Birmingham has two universities; a vast new polytechnic; a college of art and design, commerce and food; teaching hospitals; superlative libraries; and two art galleries. At the Central Reference Library there is the Shakespeare Memorial Library, one of the finest collections in the world. In the theatre and in music Birmingham has achieved con-

21

4. A Victorian court-
yard.

5. New homes for old.
Many thousands of
people were rehoused
after the war and
today Birmingham is
the largest housing
authority in the land.

siderable eminence; the Repertory Theatre and the Birmingham Symphony Orchestra enjoy world-wide fame. In sport there are such famous football teams as Birmingham City and Aston Villa, and Edgbaston is a classic cricket ground.

In all its many facets Birmingham is a city of immense enterprise and aggressive confidence. Its coat of arms, with the single word 'Forward', refers to the city's medieval origins, at the same time expressing her role as a city of European status both industrially and culturally. Some of the city's forward-looking spirit comes from the days when the great statesman Joseph Chamberlain was Mayor of Birmingham in the latter part of the nineteenth century. Today, after being a major target of German air raids during the Second World War, it has achieved an outstanding record in municipal improvements. Not only have more than ten thousand slum properties gone, but the city is in the vanguard of those now tackling the problem of bringing people back to the 'dying' inner-city areas so that once again they may be happily inhabited — not mere commercial compounds with only a daytime population. It has long ceased building multi-storey homes which proved a failure for many in terms of human health and happiness.

Now it is a very different looking city from the one I first came to over twenty years ago. I was one of the thousands of wives who lived in Birmingham because their husbands worked there. After a fruitless search for a country house within easy commuting distance we fortunately discovered Edgbaston and there made our home in a late Regency house. In one direction it was a ten-minute drive to the University (where my husband held the Chair in the Department of Anatomy); in the other it was ten minutes to the railway station. The contrast in the two drives made a strong impact on me — one was through tree-lined roads of elegant homes, the other through squalid streets of slum houses. I was deeply moved by the often bedraggled and poorly nourished children in the Victorian slums of Ladywood and Lee Bank (areas now reclaimed and rebuilt). I liked to walk about the back streets, stopping to photograph and talk to children and admiring the imaginative way they made playgrounds of old bomb sites. As my own children grew up I became involved in Birmingham local activities, particularly with the welfare of children and young people. The more I got to know about the town and its people the more I began to respect what the city stood for and the more annoyed I became at the poor image 'Brum' seemed to be saddled with outside.

Tremendous changes have taken place in the appearance of the city since we left. Sadly, many buildings of character have been destroyed. Much has been swept away that should have been treasured, and the making of new roads has become somewhat obsessional. Criticism is, however, all too easy. Birmingham is justly proud of her achievements; its houses are well designed, and good landscaping and play-grounds continue to improve the environment. Nevertheless,

6. The magnificent civic regalia of the city includes this silver cup made by T. Simpson, Birmingham, in 1813. The cup was subscribed in sixpences by the city's workers as a token of their gratitude to Thomas Attwood (see Chapter 13) 'for his constant attention to their interests'. In 1935 the cup was presented to the city by Miss E.C. Attwood.

one is sorry to see the streets of little homes demolished although I know that many were in shocking repair and offered little joy. Despite this, the community spirit in these areas was strong; family groups and lifelong friends provided good companionship and ready help in times of trouble. Furthermore, the streets of small houses fitted the town-scape, easily climbing up and down the hills in warm red brick (perhaps this was because the scale was right, leaving the eye free to wander over the rooftops towards the spires of churches and factory chimneys).

But this is no epitaph for Birmingham, for which I have a great affection. The village which has grown and overspilt and bred new townships can no longer be thought of except in the context of conurbation. It is, moreover, a city with an exceptionally rich record of human history and progress. Sir Edward Burne-Jones, the nineteenth-century Birmingham-born artist and designer of the spectacular windows in Birmingham Cathedral, forecast that 'Birmingham shall be a famous city of white stone, full of brave architecture, carved

7. This imposing new Chamber of Commerce building in Harborne Road is a centre of business life. The Chamber and the firms it represents have made a worthy contribution to the elegant Edgbaston scene.

and painted'. Let us hope that one day he will prove right, and that the best and most interesting buildings of her unique and historic past will still be there.

I think my feelings about Birmingham are common to many people and I hope that with the professional help and guidance of my Birmingham-born co-author and friend Geoffrey Eley we can share our enthusiasm with readers of this book for the outstanding part played by the city of Birmingham in the development of Great Britain and her former Empire.

Burnham Thorpe,   Joan Zuckerman
King's Lynn,   October 1978
Norfolk.

1. Spirit of Independence

Birmingham's dramatic story starts with the Boerma people — a Germanic tribe and one of the peoples known collectively as Anglo-Saxons — sailing into England from the North Sea by way of the River Trent and its tributary the Tame. In the seventh or eighth century they established a settlement in Birmingham on the banks of a small river called the Rea. Soon commerce and the working of metals began contributing to the growth of Birmingham from a village into the biggest manufacturing city in England. This phenomenal growth is surprising, since there are no metal ores in Birmingham's subsoil, and no large river or port to facilitate trade — but the early inhabitants of the sandy, sparsely vegetated area did enjoy two advantages which encouraged trading. First, the only place where the River Rea was shallow enough to ford was at the foot of the Boerma tribe's hamlet; second, as county boundaries emerged in the tenth century the settlement was fortuitously close to the point where Warwickshire, Worcestershire and Staffordshire met, so making it a natural meeting ground for a large area.

The changes brought about through succeeding centuries are best seen in roughly chronological order, the site of the original village now being covered by the Smithfield Market in Digbeth and Birmingham's famous parish church of St Martin-in-the-Bullring.

The first historically significant change came after the Norman Conquest in 1066, when Birmingham became part of a large estate comprising over eighty other manors which William the Conqueror presented to one Fitz Ansculf. The estate passed to Fitz Ansculf's daughter, who married Fulke

The first settlers

27

Pagenell, then went to their grandson, Lord of Dudley. In 1150 Peter Fitzwilliam acquired the Birmingham Manor and the title 'Lord of Bremengeham' from Lord Dudley. Manor and title remained in this family until the middle of the sixteenth century.[1]

In 1166, Henry II granted a Charter allowing weekly village markets and this provided Peter de Bremengeham with a market toll. Why Peter acquired a Charter to trade earlier than other, and larger, villages in the area remains a mystery – possibly this Charter merely legalised an already existing but irregular situation; what *is* known is that it gave Birmingham a head start.

Not content with its weekly market, a second Charter was acquired by Birmingham in the thirteenth century permitting fairs to be held. These events attracted people from far afield, many of whom stayed to become members of a prosperous and lively community. The Lord of the Manor ruled his village with a light hand, and encouraged both his 'villeins' (feudal serfs) and the new inhabitants to seek 'rights of burgage' (tenancies of land). Freed in this way from the burdens of community farming there was plenty of opportunity to develop the crafts and trades.

The Lord of Birmingham and some of the prosperous villagers raised enough money in the fourteenth century to endow a stone-built priory (St Thomas of Canterbury) and a small chapel – these first stone buildings stood where Lewis's department store is now. Not long afterwards, Peter de Bremengeham's Church (on the same site as today's parish church of St Martin) was rebuilt in stone, with the addition of a 200-foot spire. By the end of the century Birmingham had formed close links with its coal- and iron-producing neighbours, to which the city has remained faithful to the present day. This trading relationship largely came about because Birmingham was on the route of a new highway connecting Worcester with Lichfield and this encouraged ironsmiths to set up forges in Birmingham, bringing with them iron and coal from places like Halesowen, Walsall and Dudley (all today within the Birmingham conurbation). Encouragement to newcomers had its rewards for Birmingham. The village grew, commercial activities increased fast

8. Dr Joseph Priestley, a Protestant dissenter from the Established Church and pastor of the Old Meeting House, was the chief target of the Birmingham riots in 1791. The Old Meeting House and the home of Dr Priestley — a great scientist as well as churchman — were then plundered and burnt in the riots. (From the work of the British historical painter Robert Haydon 1786 — 1848.)

and by the early part of the fifteenth century there were many prosperous yeomen in Birmingham. These yeomen founded a religious organisation known as the Gild of the Holy Cross, administered by a group of well-to-do philanthropists. They built a Gild Hall on the fringe of the village (where the present-day shopping area of New Street begins) and the Hall later became the first home of the King Edward VI Grammar School. The original Gild Hall was used for meetings, public feasts and entertainments — and it possessed a chiming mechanical clock which was the timekeeper for the entire Birmingham village.

Religious gilds were responsible for all parish property as well as functioning much as an elected local authority. The Gild

Religious gilds

29

of the Holy Cross looked after the old, the sick and the needy. Almshouses were provided for twelve poor persons and the Gild maintained two bridges, one over the River Rea which today flows in a brick channel beneath the centre of the city.

The village of Birmingham ran so efficient and democratic a gild that it was not much bothered when the manorial Lord, Edward de Birmingham, was arraigned for treason in 1529. Although later pardoned, Edward never returned to Birmingham. In accordance with custom his lands reverted to the Crown, which leased them to tenants. The Manor House remained empty.

It was most unusual for a sizeable village such as Birmingham to be without either a powerful overlord (such as the Earl of Chester at Coventry) or a strong manorial Lord. Also Birmingham was without both a resident Bishop and an organised Merchant/Craft Guild, a freedom from restraint which seems to have been much to its advantage. The growing village was already showing that independence of spirit and communal strength which was to exemplify the future city's prestige.

Before deciding on the dissolution of the monastries Henry VIII sent Commissioners to report on the country's religious endowments — many of which were corrupt and inefficient. Not so Birmingham, where the Commissioners reported that 'the priests were all needed for a proper performance of the services' and that the 'social endowments were well used'. However, although it boasted a 'Free Church' (which is to say, a reformed church) in St John's, Deritend, the town priory's chanceries were in due course suppressed and the religious gilds broken up. All that was saved from the dissolution of gilds in Birmingham was 'property worth £21 a year to provide an income for the new grammar school which was housed in the Gild Hall in New Street, together with the stipend of a priest for St. John's Chapel'.

The new grammar school was founded in 1552, twelve years after Bishop Vesey of Exeter had founded a grammar school at Sutton Coldfield, his native town. The school in the city centre was twice rebuilt on the same site, but in 1936 it moved to Edgbaston. Today we know it as King Edward VI

Grammar School, one of the most illustrious of all England's academic schools and the parent of several other King Edward schools in Birmingham.

In those Tudor days most of the Manor of Birmingham was open fields and orchards, but the main road from south to north was lined with tanneries, forges and houses. In 1538 John Leland, one of the great English topographers, rode through Bordesley and Deritend on his way into Birmingham. He was charmed by Deritend which he found 'as pretty a street as I ever entered', but he was shocked by the noise made by the smiths of Birmingham. The Old Crown Inn, a gabled black and white timbered public house which, in Leland's time, stood in pleasant gardens on the Deritend bank of the river, is still in thriving business at the Bull Ring end of the Coventry Road.

The Tudor scene

9. An old smithy and open forge in Digbeth (removed early in the 19th century).

Tudor Birmingham possessed several important tanning yards; indeed its leather markets first put the town on the map. Tanners needed plenty of running water for processing raw hides into leather and Birmingham fortunately had adequate supplies of both good spring and river water. Undoubtedly, this was a major factor in promoting the town's development; another natural asset Birmingham enjoyed was the local deposits of certain special sands needed for metal moulding purposes.

The word 'smith' applied to all men who worked with metal, but many smithies specialised in particular articles. There were lorrimers, who made horse bits and spurs; cutlers, who made swords, scythes and knives; while other smiths concentrated on household articles such as milk pails, pots and pans, lanterns, kettles, fire backs and fire irons. The poorer smiths made a living out of nails and horseshoes. All the forges were open booths annexed to houses. They flanked the road at Digbeth, giving the appearance of a long stretch of open market.

Throughout the seventeenth century the town of Birmingham, despite suffering an epidemic of plague, continued to attract new inhabitants and new trades — including gunmaking. New metals, particularly brass and copper, were fast coming into favour and the metal industries were taking over from leather and wool.

There followed a serious shortage of charcoal used by the iron-makers. This caused the ironmasters of Sussex and Surrey, the original centres of the iron trade, to move towards Wales, where there was a more plentiful supply of timber available for charcoal. Birmingham smiths were not dramatically affected by the shortage as the local woodlands had escaped the wholesale destruction suffered in southern England to provide timber for ships and expanding industries such as brick and glass-making. In fact, they reaped advantages from the upheavals in the south and soon outclassed all other iron-making centres. A major factor here was the proximity of open-cast coal from Staffordshire. As charcoal supplies dwindled coal became commonly used by the smiths for coarser iron work; for delicate work charcoal remained a necessity since the carbon from coal made the iron too soft — and coke was still a fuel of the future.

Note

1. William de Bermingham was killed at the Battle of Evesham in 1265 when the Prince of Wales defeated the barons led by Simon de Montfort, Earl of Leicester, and enabled Henry III to regain the throne.

2. A Growing Influence

It was during the seventeenth century that Birmingham's commercial influence began to make itself felt both at home and overseas. However, instead of a badly needed period of stable economic growth, uninterrupted by expensive wars on the Continent, the policies of King Charles I led to frustration and — when Parliament finally turned against the King — to civil war.

There was no part of the country more violently anti-royalist than the Midlands, and to oppose King Charles — who had fled to York — the Earl of Essex raised a Parliamentary force there. In 1642, when the King attacked Coventry, his troops were defeated by the local Parliamentarians, well reinforced by men from Warwick and Birmingham. It was not, however, as fighting men that the citizens of Birmingham made their biggest contributions to the outcome of the battles of the Civil War — they were primarily the providers of weapons for the Parliamentarians. Birmingham supplied the Earl of Essex with swords and probably with pikes and muskets as well. Robert Porter, the proprietor of one large Birmingham blade mill, is said to have supplied Essex with as many as 15,000 swords.

When the King's forces prepared to launch an attack on London from their headquarters at Oxford, Prince Rupert, the King's nephew, attempted to open a supply line from Yorkshire to Oxford. He captured Lichfield and managed to 'settle there a garrison for the King'. On leaving the town he was forced to pass through Birmingham — and there ran into serious trouble. This contemporary description of the incident comes from the *History of the Great Rebellion* by

34

Edward Hyde, later Earl of Clarendon, and Chief Adviser to Charles II (at York):

> In his way thither he was to march through Birmingham a town in Warwickshire before mentioned and of as great fame for hearty wilful affected disloyalty to the King as any place in England ... the next day after his remove thence the inhabitants of that place [Birmingham] seized on his [the King's] carriages, wherein were his own plate and furniture and conveyed them to Warwick Castle [a Parliamentary stronghold] and had from that time, with unusual industry and vigilance, apprehended all messengers who were employed or suspected to be so, in the King's service. Though Birmingham was never made a garrison by direction of the Parliament, being built in such a form as was indeed hardly capable of being fortified — yet they had so great a desire to distinguish themselves from the King's good subjects that they cast a little slight works at both ends of the town, and barricaded the rest, and voluntarily engaged themselves not to admit any intercourse with the King's forces.

> In this posture Prince Rupert now found them, having in the town with them at that time a troop of horse belonging to the garrison of Lichfield, which was grown to that strength that it infested those parts exceedingly, and would in short time have extended itself to a powerful jurisdiction. His Highness, hardly believing it possible that when they should discover his power they would offer to make resistance and being unwilling to receive interruption in his more important design, sent his quarter-masters thither to take up his lodging, and to assure them that if they behaved themselves peaceably they should not suffer for what was past. But they had not consciences good enough to believe him and absolutely refused to let them quarter in the town. From their little works, with mettle equal to their malice, they discharged their shot upon him: but they were quickly over-powered, and some parts of the town being fired, they were not able to contend with both enemies, and, distracted between both, suffered the assailant to enter vengeance upon them that they deserved, but made them expiate their transgression with paying a less mulct then might have been expected from their wealth if their wickedness had been less.

Perhaps Clarendon never knew the whole story. After spending the night in Birmingham 'looting, rapeine, feasting and drinking', the cavaliers set fire to eighty houses, burnt Porter's blade mill to the ground and imposed a substantial fine upon the citizens.

Feeling against Roman Catholics ran high during the Civil War. One Catholic family was driven from their home, Edgbaston Hall (now Edgbaston Golf Club) when the house was taken by a troop raised from the small craftsmen of Birmingham under the command of Colonel 'Tinker' Fox, from Walsall. It would seem probable that 'Tinker' and his troop led the band of more than 1,000 Parliamentarians which successfully besieged Sir Thomas Holt, a distinguished Justice of the Peace and a Loyalist, at his Jacobean mansion of Aston Hall (it is still possible today to see the damage done by cannon-balls during the fight).

Ecclesiastical reforms

Birmingham actively supported the strong national movement towards expanding industrial and commercial power overseas. It sided with the pressure groups which successfully sought for a reformation within the Church. The reforms desired included suppression of all bishops (they were considered obstructive and superfluous), simplification of Church services and — most important of all — the abolition of the Divine Right of Kings (this was intended to restrict the power of a King and his Court). However, Cromwell died in 1658 and almost immediately his government began to crumble. It was only a matter of time before Charles II (son of Charles I who had been executed in 1649) was restored to the throne. In May 1660 he was declared King. Everywhere Charles II was received with enthusiasm, the nation as a whole being sick of Cromwellian military despotism and rigid Puritanism.

Politically, the Restoration of 1660 restored King, Parliament and law in place of military dictatorship and in religion it restored the bishops, the Prayer Book and Anglican beliefs in place of Puritanism. The settlement was not followed by any great persecution of Cromwell's supporters, but the new tolerance did not extend to all religious matters. Whilst most of the landed aristocracy rallied to the new King, thereby retaining their rank and property, the middle-class men of

commerce were reluctant to see the old order re-established. Above all, these merchants and traders wished to have an influential voice in the country's planning policies. Many refused to accept the re-established Church of England and so became, by their refusal to conform to an established order, Nonconformists or Dissenters.

Dissenters became so numerous and so troublesome that severe restrictions were imposed on them by Parliament. The 1662 Act of Uniformity drove large numbers of Dissenting ministers, Roman Catholics included, out of their livings. Attendance at religious meetings, other than those of the Church of England, was totally forbidden. Three years later an Act which became known as the Five Mile Act made it illegal for a Dissenting clergyman, or a schoolmaster, to appear within a five-mile radius of any corporate town. Simultaneously, all positions in national or local government, and commissions in the army, were closed to anyone other than a practising member of the Church of England.

Restrictions on Dissenters

There were many Dissenters who gave up the fight and became members of the Church of England. But others stood firm, among them some early Presbyterian Nonconformists, a number of whom lived in Birmingham. Because it was unincorporated, the town was free from some of the most tiresome religious restrictions. For this reason many neighbouring Dissenters preferred to move to Birmingham. By 1700 there were two congregations of Presbyterians, and a meeting house for Quakers.[1]

The rise
of science

The Restoration world was, even so, less preoccupied with religion than Cromwellian England and, instead, encouraged the spread of experimental science and manufacturing trade. It was at this time of change that the Royal Society — Britain's oldest scientific society — was founded under the patronage of King Charles II. Although another hundred years were to pass before the Industrial Revolution, scientific thought and invention in seventeenth-century England was being increasingly applied to manufacturing processes — not least in Birmingham, where some practising scientists as well as craftsmen lived and worked.

During the second half of the century Birmingham's population trebled in size. This huge increase — from 5,000 to 15,000 inhabitants — made Birmingham the industrial centre of the Midlands and brought her to the top of the league of provincial towns. Birmingham overtook Manchester and other Lancashire towns whose importance was rising fast with the growth of the weaving industry.

Note

1. Quakers spread through Europe, mostly from Germany. Between 1647 and 1661 many were imprisoned and some were put to death in England, and also in America, where they finally became accepted in 1670.

3. 'Toyshop of Europe'

Trade was booming by the early years of the eighteenth century, and much-needed improvements were made in road and river transport. Better transport helped the movement of coal and certainly assisted in bringing down the cost of Britain's finished articles for sale. It was about this time that Birmingham merchants started to specialise. Some concerned themselves only with marketing, some produced their own iron, with which they fed their own furnaces, forges and mills. Others became middlemen, lending money and providing raw materials to smiths and artisans. The blade mills — such as the Sarehole Mill and Pebble Mill on the Bourne brook — specialised in the grinding of sharp edges, and the cutting-tool trade became specialised, concerning itself with the manufacture of swords, daggers, scissors, knives and razors.

The boom in trade

To keep down costs Birmingham smiths experimented with different mixtures of metals, and this added to the variety of their products — nails, for instance, became a staple industry of the town. So were domestic utensils such as pots and pans, ladles and fish-slices, candlesticks and 'pricks' (pricks were wall brackets with an upward shaft to hold rush or tallow candles). Brass (an alloy of copper and zinc) was favoured for decorative work as it was softer than iron and easier to shape; small articles were frequently moulded in casts.[1]

Large wrought-iron items such as chimney cranes for kitchens were now being made, but probably only for local use. Some of the kitchen cranes made in the late seventeenth and early eighteenth centuries were able to move in two or three planes, so that cooking-pots could be hung at different

A nursery of skills

39

heights over any part of an open fire. Another piece of contemporary kitchen machinery which came in at this time was the spit-jack, a giant wrought-iron skewer on which the meat rotated over the fire. Developing these kitchen instruments required an understanding of problems relating to heat and draughts and mathematical calculations for devising weights and pulleys. Thus Birmingham became a nursery for many skills which matured in the later Industrial Revolution.

The Restoration was a period of inventive ability. Birmingham became established in a leading position in the manufacture of metal buttons (the first patent for which was taken out in 1631), shoe-fastening buckles (first worn in the reign of Charles II), guns (later Birmingham was to become, at least for a time, the supplier of almost every firearm sold in England or exported from it), and 'toys' (a comprehensive term for any useful lightweight manufactured article). Birmingham was about to earn the title of 'the toyshop of Europe' — this description (meaning essential hardware, *not* toys, as we understand the word) was first used in the House of Commons in 1777 by the Irish statesman Edmund Burke.

Centre of button-making

To encourage trade in metal buttons an Act of Parliament was passed forbidding the import of foreign buttons (mostly French and made of mohair). This was followed by a ban on imported cotton-covered buttons. Masses of brass buttons for uniforms and liveries were made in Birmingham, and before long Birmingham became the button-making centre for all England. Exporting buttons also became big business — there is a record of a shipment of military brass buttons going to Russia at the end of the eighteenth century.

The Birmingham manufacture of guns (see Chapter 10) and 'toys' is of particular interest in the city's history because both played a highly important part in the industrial expansion of the following century. 'Toys', roughly classed as 'light steel toys' and 'heavy steel toys', included fire-shovels, pokers and tongs (hardly 'toys' as we now understand the word!) and eventually this manufacture developed into the cheap jewellery trade. Brooches, bracelets, rings, watch-chains, hatpins and a huge variety of small decorated boxes, including many thousands of snuff-boxes, were made in

40

Birmingham. A century ago the city's yearly output of wedding-rings was over 50,000 and jewellery is still one of Birmingham's important industries.

In 1728 Daniel Defoe, author of *Robinson Crusoe*, sang the praises of Birmingham brass and copper goods. In his *Plan of the English Commerce* he wrote that articles made of brass and copper were being sold all over Europe and in the Levant (originally the general name given to the East) and that they were becoming even more popular than French metal goods. There were, however, besides Birmingham, other sources of 'toys' in the Midlands, as J.U. Nef relates in *The Rise of the British Coal Industry*:

> An early eighteenth-century traveller wandering from Birmingham to Wolverhampton, and thence to Stourbridge by way of Walsall, must have been amazed to find that inhabitants everywhere were employed in industry, for the 'Black Country' had already taken on its characteristic aspect. Here were collieries, glass works, lime, brick, and malt kilns in abundance; but the fame of the district rested upon the manufacture of every sort of iron, copper, and brass ware. Every farm has one forge or more; so that the farmers carry on two very different businesses, working at their forges as smiths, when they are not employed in the fields as farmers. And all their work they bring to market where the great tradesmen buy it up and send to London.

The trade of the smith was not, of course, a new one. William Camden had found Birmingham 'swarming with inhabitants, and echoing with the noises of anvils'.

Birmingham smiths kept down their prices, and the weight of finished articles, by mixing together a variety of metals (for instance, covering iron cores with tinplate for door handles) and the practice outraged the London-based smiths. There was deeply felt grievance and Birmingham smiths were accused by London of marketing goods that were 'falsely and deceitfully made'. In spite of this, the Midlands never gave up trading with London. The reputation of Birmingham was based on highly finished and delicate metal work. By this time the less skilful smiths, such as the nail-makers, had left the town to be nearer their supplies of raw materials.

41

11. Birmingham has every kind of public house and the oldest building remaining in the city centre is a pub. The Old Crown in High Street, Deritend, was built by Robert O'Greene in 1368. (See p. 157.)

Thus is the stage set for the rise of many illustrious names in industry and science, from early in the eighteenth century to the present day; for the advance of industrial steam power and transport by railway; and for the first purpose-built factory unit in the world, the renowned Soho Works of Matthew Boulton.

Note

1. The copper-mining monopoly which kept a stranglehold on supply and prices was smashed in 1689 to the great benefit of Birmingham, which used an increasing amount of straight copper, mixing this with calamine (a fine ore) to transform it to brass.

42

4. The Princely Boulton

The National Exhibition Centre at Birmingham is a fitting memorial to the pioneering of those early scientists and inventive manufacturers whose names and achievements are part of Birmingham's heritage. It was to Edward Thomason, son of one of these remarkable manufacturers, that the idea first came for making the name of Birmingham better known in Europe. The story goes that an Austrian gentleman, visiting the city towards the end of the eighteenth century, declared that he had never heard of the place before — and Thomason decided to put matters right. He was well qualified for the task; not only was he son of a Birmingham businessman making a thousand buckles a day, but he had served an apprenticeship with the famous Matthew Boulton at the Soho Works before becoming an inventor and diplomat — proud to boast that he was vice-consul to eight foreign countries.

To project the name of Birmingham throughout Europe, Thomason designed a series of sixty expensive large medals showing scenes from the Bible and he sent one of these to every monarch in Europe. The fine craftsmanship did more than boost the image of Birmingham. It won for Edward Thomason a collection of eight knighthoods, including one bestowed by William IV, King of England.

By the early part of the eighteenth century Birmingham had become the home of an ever-growing number of notable manufacturers whose work brought an increasing international reputation to the town. Among the outstanding early names were those of John Taylor and Sampson Lloyd, both Quakers and very prosperous manufacturers. Taylor's

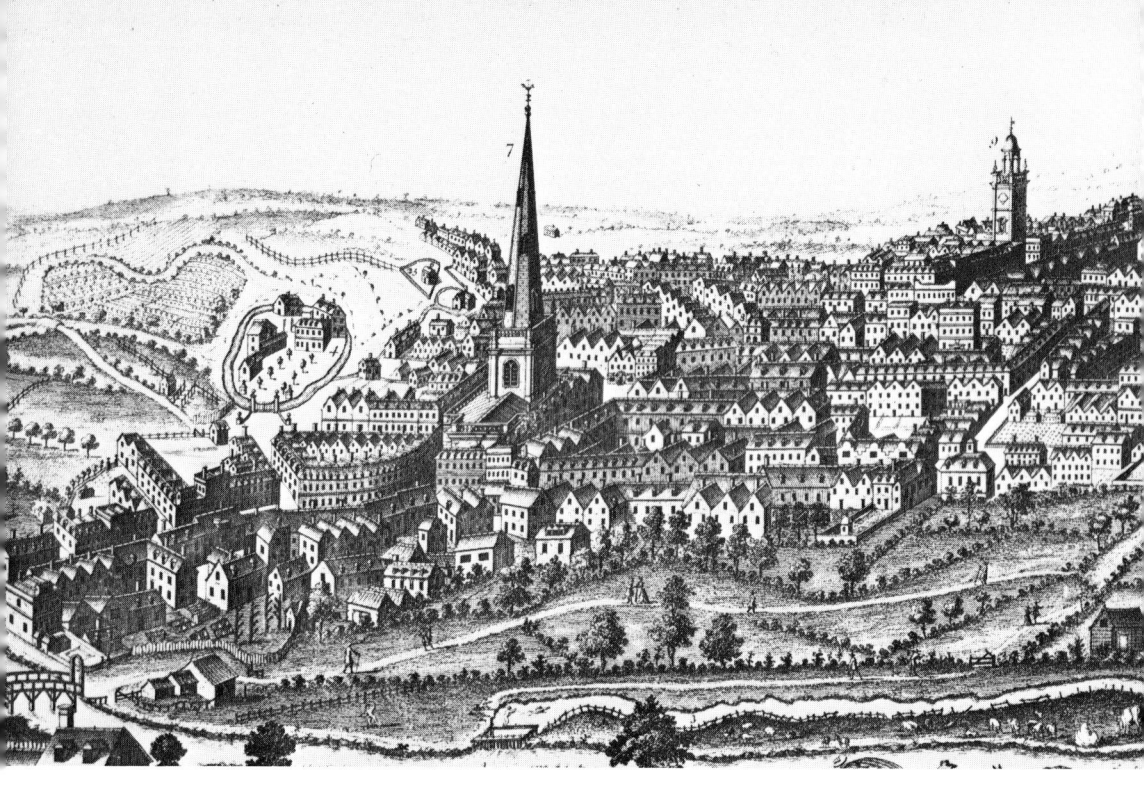

12. A section of Westley's 1730 print 'The East Prospect of Birmingham' showing St Martin's Church behind the River Rea and open land in the foreground. Westley described his subject as 'a market town in the county of Warwick which, by the art and industry of its inhabitants, has been rendered famous all over the world for the rare choice and invention of all sorts of wares'.

business was chiefly buckle- and button-making; with the help of large numbers of outside, semi-skilled craftsmen he also made many varieties of 'toys' and decorative articles using ivory, tortoiseshell, pearl and silver. His contemporary, Sampson Lloyd, was a wealthy steel merchant with his own slitting mill where heavy iron was slit into thin rods.

The city's first bank

These pioneers Taylor and Lloyd combined to establish the first joint-stock bank in Birmingham and by so doing fathered the famous bank of today bearing Lloyd's name. The first bank, although limited in its capacity to give credit, was of the utmost benefit to Birmingham's expanding industry — particularly since the raising of money had become very difficult and time-consuming at a national level,

44

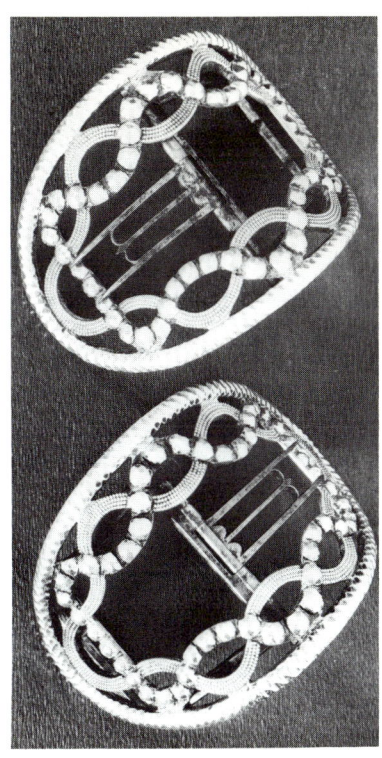

13. & 14. In the first half of the 18th century buckle and button making were important Birmingham trades. This collection of 500 buttons was made by James Luckcock, a local jeweller. It includes pearl buttons, one of the city's most profitable exports. The silver shoe buckles are from the Birmingham Assay Office collection.

for bills of debt could be negotiated only in the most complicated manner and the aristocracy were 'living it up' on credit to the detriment of the city's merchants and traders.

Even the outstanding Birmingham-born engineer Matthew Boulton was among those constantly bedevilled by lack of funds. When he was 31 Matthew Boulton took over his father's button and buckle business but soon endangered this by investing too much of his earnings into workshop buildings and debts mounted. Only through the help of his friends Taylor and Lloyd did the young Boulton eventually succeed in bringing James Watt into partnership to develop the newly invented steam engines for commercial use. The name of James Watt is connected with steam power, and how he first got the idea from watching the steam lift the lid of a boiling kettle is known to every man and child. Not so well known is the part he played with Matthew Boulton, the more business-like member of the partnership, whom Watt himself described as 'the princely Boulton'.

Boulton and the Soho Works

Matthew Boulton's move to Soho from his father's button business largely came about as a result of his two marriages into a wealthy Lichfield family, the Robinsons. In 1756, when Matthew was 28, he married Anne Robinson, who brought with her a dowry of £28,000. Three years later Anne died and Matthew subsequently married her sister, adding so much to his financial standing that he could have retired had he wished. Boulton, however, had plans for business expansion at Soho and for adding still further lustre to the name of Birmingham as an international workshop.

First he commissioned a local architect Samuel Wyatt (brother of James Wyatt, an eminent Italian-trained architect) to design a factory on the Soho site near Hockley brook — a geographical feature of the district which was to have industrial significance later. He then took into partnership John Fothergill, a man experienced in marketing at home and abroad.

The Soho Works became a showpiece, visitors from far and wide coming to see the innovations made by Boulton. Within the factory each 'shop' concentrated on one single process — an imaginative leap into what in our present time has become

46

15. & 16. The Soho
Works of Matthew
Boulton and James
Watt opened in 1762. It
soon became Europe's
finest example of
advanced engineering
skill. Here James Watt
perfected the steam
engine. The 1777
engine (see below) was
made for pumping
water for the
Birmingham Canal
Company and is now
preserved at the city's
Science Museum.
Part of the original
Soho building,
including machines
installed in the late
18th century, is pre-
served by Avery's, the
weighing machine
makers.

normal large-scale production technique. As it does now, the article being made circulated around the factory for different processes and the workers stayed put. Boulton's then revolutionary changes paid off. He was soon a large employer of men, women and children, each with their allotted task. Within ten years from the time he bought the Soho site, with its modest water-mill, Boulton's renowned works consisted of four squares of large buildings with workshops for over a thousand operatives. His home, called Soho House, was described as 'the resort of lords and ladies, princes and philosophers, servants and students to a far greater extent than many European courts'.[1]

Boulton, wise and careful in his choice of staff, gathered around himself many able people. On one occasion, when William Murdoch, the inventor of gas lighting, went to the Soho Works looking for a job, Boulton saw him but, apparently, was not impressed. He was about to turn him away when the nervous Murdoch dropped his hat, which made an odd noise as it fell on the office floor. When asked why the hat made such a noise Murdoch explained to Boulton that he had made the hat from wood, having discovered a technique for turning an oval object on a lathe. Murdoch was instantly given a job at Soho, at fifteen shillings a week!

A model
for others

When the Soho buildings — carefully sited to take advantage of the new London to Chester road — were finally completed in 1762 they formed the world's first purpose-designed factory for making metal goods and served as a model for many others in later years. Boulton's methods increased output tenfold over the average at that time. Everything that could be of any use was harnessed to production. The Hockley brook, by means of a short connecting canal, was made to power two new water-mills turning machines for rolling, polishing, grinding and operating lathes. So that he could recycle metal scrap into cast iron, and convert iron into steel, Boulton built his own steelhouse (one of Birmingham's main thoroughfares is known as Steelhouse Lane). There poured from the Soho Works an ever-growing volume of die-stamping and pressing, and brass-founding, including the casting of taps and machine parts, door handles, carriage fittings, candlesticks and lamps of all kinds.

Meanwhile, in London, Boulton set up a warehouse and issued an illustrated catalogue of mass-produced prefabricated parts such as teapot spouts, silver handles, feet and knobs for dishes and jugs, cut-steel sword hilts and ormolu mounts.[2] Boulton worked hard in London to persuade people of fashion to buy his goods, holding sales at Christie's showrooms in Pall Mall and publicising these sales around the coffee-houses in Town. For one sale alone he sent out fifteen thousand invitations. Boulton's sales organisation extended overseas and included an agent who represented both Boulton and the world-famous Staffordshire pottery designer Josiah Wedgwood at the Court of Queen Catherine II of Russia. Wedgwood ware and Boulton silver candlesticks can be seen today by visitors to the Leningrad Palace.

Boulton was determined to have his silverware hallmarked in Birmingham so that it did not have to travel to Chester or London. He used his influence to get an Act of Parliament passed permitting an Assay Office for Birmingham (in Britain almost all articles of gold and silver have to be hallmarked, which guarantees that the amount of precious metal used meets the required standard). There was, of course, opposition to Boulton's plans from the London silversmiths but this he overcame and from 1773 to the present day the Assay Office of Birmingham has hallmarked silver and gold with its famous anchor symbol.

While his marketing expert John Fothergill was energetically selling overseas, at home in Birmingham Boulton was ever exploring new forms of manufacture, or finding out about other people's secret processes! In this manner he turned his inquiring mind to the making of Sheffield plate and before long the Soho Works became the only factory outside Sheffield to produce it.[3]

Collectors' pieces

When Boulton made Sheffield plate and ormolu he not only borrowed and bought works of art but himself employed artists to adapt these works and designs for Soho-made shapely candelabra, delicate ornaments, clocks and exquisite snuff-boxes for the nobility and royalty. Many of Boulton's articles are collectors' pieces today — just as Sheffield plate, once considered as the poor man's silver, is today justly

50

17. Some fine examples of Birmingham silverware, hallmarked MB, made at Matthew Boulton's Soho Works. (Top) An epergne and basket; (below) a pair of tureens dated 1773 and an egg frame.

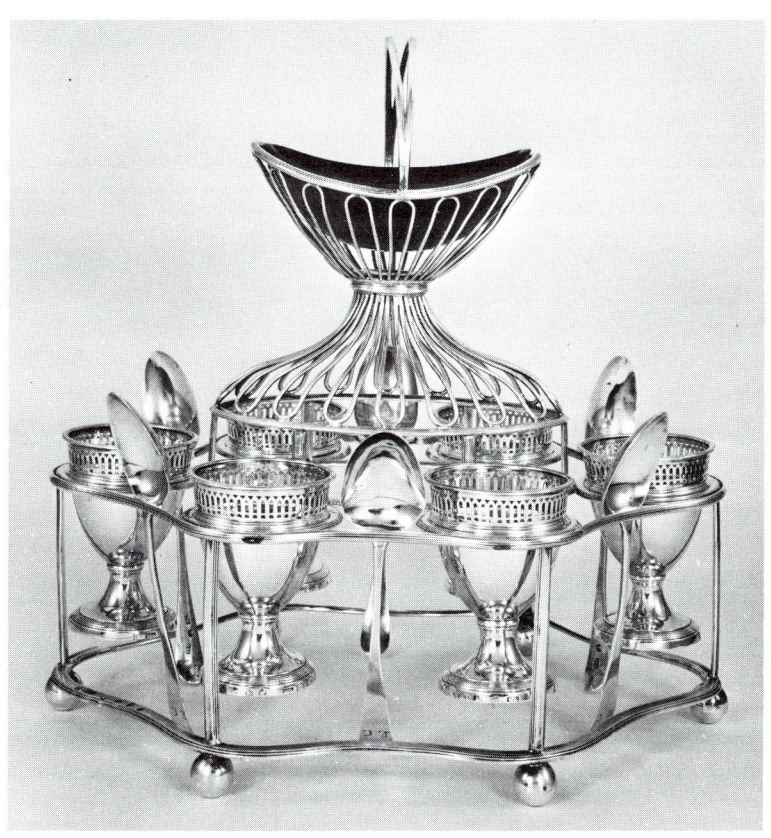

prized for its own sake. And no one made better Sheffield plate than Matthew Boulton at Soho.

Besides being such an inventive manufacturer, Boulton as a man of outstanding personality, vision and enthusiasm — the princely Boulton indeed — made many useful social contacts. His friends were men of power and influence, men like Josiah Wedgwood, some of whose precious-stone cameos were mounted in ormolu at Soho. When Boulton died in 1809, aged 81, six hundred of his workers attended his funeral at Handsworth. It cost over £2,000 and each Soho worker was provided with a hatband, gloves and a silver medal and, after the burial, a lavish dinner.

Hard work and hard play

The age of Matthew Boulton and James Watt was not, however, only a time of accelerating industrial momentum. In Birmingham, craftsmen were bubbling over with new inventions and stepping up output by every means they could think of — but though these townspeople were so exceptionally hard-working they played just as hard. There was prize-fighting, cock-fighting, fives and quoits, skittles and ale for the factory workers; horse-racing through the narrow streets and bull-baiting in the central Bull Ring for the general public (Birmingham later became the first English town to ban bull-baiting); and for the wealthy merchants there were music festivals in Duddleston Hall, held to raise money to build a general hospital; tea and bowls in private gardens; and — for those who liked travel and excitement — a flying coach to London Town (journey time 2½ days!)

Wool-spinning invention

The city's early inventions include one in the name of John Wyatt, 'as of Birmingham, gentleman'. In 1738 he took out a patent for a 'new invented machine or engine for the spinning of wool and cotton'. Thanks to John Wyatt[4] and his colleagues, Birmingham was thus the cradle of the idea of spinning by rollers which brought fame to Richard Arkwright and laid the foundation on which the cotton-spinning wealth and fame of Manchester was built. For John Wyatt himself, however, it was a sad story. He failed to get commercial recognition of his inventions (which included a file-cutting machine). Later, Wyatt got employment at Boulton's Soho Works. There he invented a double-headed lathe with lever motion for cutting pearl buttons and button moulds, metal

18. Elegant, dainty trinkets in coloured enamel were made between 1750 and the end of the 18th century. Although often called Battersea enamels, after the factory where the trade started, they were mostly made in Birmingham and surrounding districts. The chief items were boxes such as those shown here for snuff, or for sweets, tea and tobacco.

a

b

19. Trade tokens were originally introduced in the late 18th century to make good a shortage of small change in the 'regal' coinage issued by the Crown.
(a) show John Freeth, a Birmingham poet who kept a tavern in Bell Street.
(b) is a token illustrating a coin press. (c) one of the Lichfield Street workhouse

screws for wood-working and, according to some authorities, the ball-bearing.

A 'consumers' association'

What appears to have been the very first 'consumers' association' also had its origin in Birmingham. In the 1870s difficulties in securing a good supply of copper at a reasonable price led the manufacturer John Taylor, together with Matthew Boulton and a group of independent Birmingham workshop owners, to form a company to provide their own raw material. First known as the Birmingham Metal Company, its name was later changed to the Mining and Copper Company. It looked after the interests of its consumer members with guaranteed shares of the metal produced. The company erected a brass foundry alongside the Birmingham Canal.[5]

A neighbouring smelting works gave its name to Brasshouse Passage (now between Broad Street and the canal) where some of the houses of the brassfounders still stand — an attractive symbol of Birmingham as the centre, then and now, of the brass industry of England. The early brass-workers, it was noted, could be distinguished from other

54

c

d

pennies which were exempt from the Act of George III suppressing the use of
tokens after 1815. (d) a token made in Birmingham for the Anglesey copper
mines (not to scale).

workers by the green colour which coated their clothes, their
faces and their hair.

Towards the end of the eighteenth century the country's
coinage was in a highly unsatisfactory state. A shortage had
given rise to a spate of counterfeit coins, most of which were
thought to be the work of Birmingham metal-smiths;
counterfeit coins became known nation-wide as Birmingham
Halfpence. Though the making of counterfeit coinage was a
capital offence, it must have proved a very profitable sideline
since it did not stop, despite the public showing of a number
of skeletons of convicted coiners 'dangling from gibbets on
Handsworth Heath'.

The shortage of coins caused difficulties in paying wages so
that many people received their pay in what were called
Tokens. These were privately minted coins and were, in
effect, sold IOUs. During 1797 over 700 tons of copper were
made into four thousand different varieties of Tokens, almost
all in Birmingham.

It was Boulton and Watt who put an end to the situation

The start of coinage

55

when they invented a new steam-powered coin press. At the Soho Works in 1786 copper coins were made for the East India Company and the American colonies, followed by silver coins for Sierra Leone. By 1797, and following the spate of Token coinage, the first English copper penny was struck at the Soho Mint. The coins were made to the exact weight of one ounce (28.35 grams) and were popularly known as Soho Pennies. Handsome commemoration medals were also designed and made at Soho, a Birmingham skill maintained today at the Birmingham Mint.

Birmingham's famous Mint

The Birmingham Mint has the longest history of any mint in the world. In 1794 a Birmingham family named Heaton opened a brass foundry in Slaney Street. By 1819 all five sons had joined their father and the firm was busy turning out not only brassware but also a range of mechanical engineering products. The Heaton family began minting coinage in 1851, using the presses and machines previously operated by Boulton and Watt at the Soho Mint. It was the beginning of a story of pioneering new processes and developing minting technology which gives the Birmingham Mint of today its outstanding world-wide reputation.

The Mint's first contract in 1851 was for the half and one centavo coins for Chile. In 1853 came its first British government contract, for 500 tons of copper pennies, halfpennies, farthings, half-farthings and quarter-farthings. Today the Birmingham Mint makes coins for over one hundred countries from, alphabetically, Australia to Zanzibar. From 1860, when the Mint moved to its present site in Icknield Street, to 1919, many Birmingham-made coins bore the company's own mark — a letter H, the founder's surname initial.

Among the new trades of the early nineteenth century was the making of pens with steel nibs. These nibs made clerical work easier and quicker and so replaced the use of goose quills. Josiah Mason,[6] who worked in a buckle-maker's shop in Birmingham, found a way of stamping out metal pen-nibs. With the help of a London businessman who sold the nibs Mason built up such a large business that Birmingham became the centre of the trade. By 1866 Mason and another maker named Joseph Gillott (a great friend of William Turner, the

56

20. A clock at Windsor Castle is reproduced here by gracious permission of Her Majesty the Queen. The clock was designed by Sir William Chambers RA. Its case, of ormolu with panels of Blue John (a Derbyshire fluorescent spar), was made by Matthew Boulton in Birmingham c. 1771. The movement of this handsome piece was by Thomas Wright.

20b. A silver shield copied (c. 1840) by the electrotype process (invented by Elkington of Birmingham) from Vechte's original which belonged to the King of Prussia.

painter) were turning out hundreds of thousands of pen-nibs every week. (See also Chapter 16.)

Yet another specialised craft, with its Birmingham-made products seen in every part of the world, is the manufacture of scales and all types of scientific and industrial weighing instruments. The firm of W. & T. Avery was founded as early as 1730 and in 1897 was transferred from its original site to the Soho Works. The management of this historic firm has always made its policy[7] clear to workers and customers alike and it is one which could be said to sum up the attitude which made Birmingham so great a city —

Weighing the world

We must work in co-operation; we must buy discreetly; produce so that others will say to us 'you made better than you know'; sell to the capacity of our production; give service to all the world.

57

Notes

1. *Dictionary of Birmingham*, first published by Walter Showell & Sons, Cross Wells Brewery, Oldbury, 1885. Reprinted by EP Publishing Ltd, Wakefield, 1969.

2. Ormolu is a superior relative of brass. It is similar to bronze in appearance, but the alloy contains only half as much tin as bronze.

3. Sheffield plate is made by coating copper with a thin layer of silver and rolling in heat until the silver flows and 'mixes' with the copper.

4. This John Wyatt was not a relative of the architects Samuel and James Wyatt referred to earlier, but is an ancester of Woodrow Wyatt, former MP for Aston.

5. Birmingham used nearly 2,000 tons of copper each year by 1790 — about a third of the total output of the Cornish copper mines.

6. Sir Josiah Mason, as he became, endowed the city's first Science College (see Chapter 16).

7. *Weighing the World* (W. & T. Avery Ltd, Soho Foundry, 1930).

5. Steam Engine Development

Boulton's Soho factory housed a lot of machinery dependent for power upon the Hockley brook. When the brook froze or dried up the water-wheel generating power came to a standstill. A Savery engine[1] was tried out unsuccessfully and Boulton, with great foresight, brought James Watt to Birmingham and financed the building of two full-size steam engines.[2] Watt had already made some headway in developing his engine under the sponsorship of a Dr John Roebuck FRS,[3] an industrial chemist. However, Roebuck ran out of funds and Boulton took over the sponsorship of Watt. Writing in *The Advancement of Science*, March 1951, W.K.V. Gale gives a clear account of the development of Watt's engine:

The need for steam

> In 1775 Watt obtained a 25-year extension of his original patent for the separate condenser, and in the same year he entered into partnership with Boulton to develop the new engine. The partnership was to last for the duration of the patent, that is 25 years. The first step was to get Watt's experimental engine from Scotland and set it to work at Soho, pumping tail-race water back into the mill pond for re-use. A standard form of engine was quickly evolved and only a year after the partnership had been formed the new firm concluded the erection of its first two engines.
>
> It is now time to say something about the features which made the Watt engine so superior to its immediate predecessor, the Newcomen. Illustrations of the two reveal very little difference in appearance, and Watt's engine could still only effect reciprocating motion. What, then, was the difference? It was simple but effective. Watt, in

21a. The interior of
Watt's workshop.

the study of the Newcomen model, had concluded that
since the cylinder was first heated by hot steam, then
cooled by cold water, again heated and so on, there
must be a tremendous loss of heat at every stroke, which
could only be made up by burning more coal. In this he
was absolutely right, and here was the explanation of the
enormous coal consumption of the Newcomen engine
compared with the work it did — in short, the reason for
its inefficiency.

Watt devised a separate condenser, kept the cylinder
permanently hot by means of a hollow casing filled with
live steam from the boiler, and obtained a permanent
cooling effect of the condenser by immersing it in a
cistern of cold water. By this means the heat losses were
greatly reduced. A little attention to detail improved
matters further, and before long a Watt engine was doing
as much work as a Newcomen with only a quarter of the
fuel. It is interesting to note that Watt's conclusions were
reached by theoretical means (as he has himself recorded)
and verified by practical experiment, actions fully in
accord with recognised practice today.

The first two engines built by the partners were installed locally. One went to Bloomfield, Tipton, for pumping water from a colliery, the other to Willey near Broseley, Shropshire, where it was used to blow a blast furnace. Here was another new departure. The growing iron trade had need for steam power, and this was only the first of many engines supplied for iron working.

The blast furnace engine was to the order of John Wilkinson, the celebrated eighteenth century ironmaster, who had also invented an improved boring machine. The business connection was to the mutual advantage of Wilkinson and the Soho partners. One of the great problems of the day was to bore a large cylinder accurately, and Wilkinson's boring mill went a great way towards providing a solution. The cylinders for both the first two engines were made by Wilkinson (in the case of his own engine he made everything else as well, to Watt's design) and for many years he continued to supply all the Boulton and Watt cylinders, Soho being responsible for the design, and the more difficult parts, such as valves and valve gear.

The first two Watt engines have long since disappeared, but in 1777 an engine was built which still exists. Erected at Smethwick for pumping water for the Birmingham Canal Company, it worked on its original site until 1895. Three years later it was removed to the Canal workshops at Ocker Hill, Tipton, for preservation.[4]

Before the partnership had been in being long, a third famous name was added to the Soho group — that of William Murdoch. Born in Scotland in 1754 Murdoch had made his way to Soho on foot in search of work, and was engaged as the firm's engine erector and agent in the field. He remained a trusted and worthy employee for many years, until he retired in 1830. The engagement of Murdoch was of great importance to the firm, for the fact that they now had an able lieutenant gave Boulton time to concentrate on commercial matters, and enabled Watt to devote his energies to research and development.

The immediate problems of pumping and furnace blowing having been settled, the pressing need was for an engine which would turn rotating machinery directly, without the use of a water-wheel, and so could be used where there was no water power.

Watt was not the only one to recognise the fact that rotative motion was urgently needed; Boulton pressed him to produce a rotative engine. 'The people are steam-mill mad', he wrote on one occasion, and even while Watt was at work, in 1780, a Newcomen engine was equipped with a crank, which enabled it to turn the stones of a flour mill. The engineer, Wasborough, of Bristol, and the mill owner Pickard, of Birmingham, obtained a patent for the use of the crank, and thus forestalled any move which Watt may have proposed to make in this direction. He might perhaps have been accused of being slow, for the crank was well-known long before his time, but this slowness was justified, for when his rotative engine did come out, in 1782, it was a great advance over the Newcomen adaptation. He overcame the crank patent with his ingenious sun and planet motion, which was used successfully for many years.

Watt's engine of 1782 was double acting — that is steam was applied to both sides of the piston, instead of to one side only as in all previous engines, and it was also worked expansively, which produced further economies in working. The rocking beam was retained, but at the cylinder end, where formerly the connections between the beam and the piston rod had been made by a chain, an alternative was necessary, because there was now an upward push on the piston as well as a downward pull. Watt at first used a known method, a rack on the piston rod working into a toothed sector on the end of the beam. It worked, and it produced the desired effect, but it was a crude and clumsy device, and wholly unsatisfactory to a man of Watt's turn of mind.

In the place of the rack and sector Watt introduced, in 1784, his celebrated parallel motion. It was a simple and effective arrangement of links, which, while permitting the end of the beam to move in an arc, restricted the movement of the piston rod within the necessary vertical line. I have been asked why Watt did not use the crosshead and slide, which became the common device some years later. He may have thought of it; I do not know, but if he had it is very doubtful if he could have obtained machinery to make it at the time. On the other hand the parallel motion gear could be produced without difficulty on the machines of the day.

The state of perfection to which the steam engine had been brought by Watt, and the fact that it was now available for such a multitude of duties, meant that the Soho partnership had more than enough to do. By 1794 the sons of the original partners, Matthew Boulton and James Watt, were taking an active part in the business.

No other place in Britain, nor in Europe, could have provided Watt with the same facilities and experience that he found at the Soho factory in Birmingham. In 1796, with the whole Soho factory, including a coin mint, working away to full capacity, Boulton and Watt decided to get the total production of steam engines under their own control by establishing their own foundry on the canal bank at Smethwick. Boulton and Watt engines were works of art and

63

visitors came from far afield to see the showpiece factory — the founding of which is often taken as the starting point of the Industrial Revolution.

Notes

1. The patent for a steam engine designed by Thomas Savery was taken out in 1698. It was primarily intended for raising water from flooded mines but was never a great success.

2. Watt's workshop was removed from Birmingham in 1924 and installed in the Science Museum at South Kensington, London, where it can be viewed.

3. Dr Roebuck was at one time a Birmingham physician. He became the first consultant chemist in Midland history and, with Samuel Garbett, built a large laboratory in Steelhouse Lane for metal-refining and the making of sulphuric acid.

4. This, the oldest steam engine in the world, remained there until 1959, when it was taken to Birmingham Science Museum. It has been kept in store for some years but it is now intended to have the engine put on public display. There is also a full-scale model of Watt's engine in the Science Museum at South Kensington.

6. The Great Baskerville

Great as the triumphs of the art of printing have been, and numerous as are the laurels which Birmingham has won, there are few nobler characters in our local story than those which record how, in a material and commercial way, John Baskerville made our town famous throughout the civilised world for the production of the best and greatest works of man, in a style which has rarely been equalled and has never been surpassed.

This summing up of the art of printing in Birmingham and, in particular, of the great type designer John Baskerville, was written by Samuel Timmins, an early Birmingham businessman, scholar and historian. Today, more than two centuries later, men of letters and printers the world over are familiar with the elegant type-face designed by Baskerville (the type you are reading in this book is a Baskerville face).

The city's greatest typographer was a colourful and eccentric character. He was born in 1706 in a Worcestershire village near Birmingham and started his working life as a footman in family service. His ambition was, however, to put his artistic abilities to good use and so decided to open a writing school in Birmingham's Bull Ring. It was highly successful but hardly the kind of occupation to satisfy another of Baskerville's ambitions — to make money.

Like so many others who have become rich, Baskerville was in the right place at the right time, and he was an opportunist. Around 1740 a new fashion for black gloss lacquer work, known as japanning, came to England and Baskerville decided to enter the trade. Again he was successful. His

Printing in Birmingham

65

artistic talent and commercial flair enabled him to produce a popular range of items such as trays and other articles for the home, snuff-boxes, panels for coach doors and much else. It is claimed that his improved techniques were such that John Baskerville revolutionised the japanning trade and earned himself a fortune in so doing.

An important Birmingham trade was started by Henry Clay, one of Baskerville's apprentices. He invented an offshoot of japanning using pasted and heated panels. His process later became popularly known as papiermâché.

Before he was forty Baskerville not only had his own carriage and pair but also a mansion (he called it Easy Hill) in Birmingham's famous Broad Street. Looking at the thronged and commercially busy Broad Street of today how odd seems the 1788 sale advertisement for the house Baskerville bought: 'the estate consists of about seven acres of rich Pasture Land in high condition, Part of which is laid out in Shady Walks, adorned with Shrubberies, Fish Ponds and a Grotto.'

John Baskerville's coach, with its beautifully pictured panels acting as 'the pattern card' of his trade, was a spectacular example of the art of japanning. It was drawn by a pair of cream-coloured horses, the master himself adding to the splendour and, incidentally, to the pleasure of the townspeople by appearing in flamboyant dress adorned with much gold lace.

Having made the fortune he sought in trade, Baskerville wished for eminence as a thinker and artist.

An artistic
fount of type

More than one of his contemporaries called him a coxcomb; and such sight as we can get of this little Voltaire of the Midlands with his naive rationalism, his churlishness in controversy and his extravagant clothes and carriage, suggests they were right. His ability as an artist in letter-forms was, however, quite another matter.[1]

At the time when Baskerville was a writing master in the Bull Ring his alphabets had been influenced by a new style of lettering developed by, among others, George Shelley, in whose *Alphabets in All Hands* (c.1715) it was well displayed. Novel characteristics of the style lay in an increase of contrast

The BOOK of
Common Prayer,

And Adminiſtration of the

SACRAMENTS,

AND OTHER

RITES and CEREMONIES

OF THE

CHURCH,

According to the Uſe of

The CHURCH of ENGLAND:

TOGETHER WITH THE

PSALTER

OR

PSALMS of DAVID,

Pointed as they are to be ſung or ſaid in Churches.

CAMBRIDGE,
Printed by JOHN BASKERVILLE, Printer to the Univerſity;
by whom they are ſold, and by B. DOD, Bookſeller,
in Ave-Mary Lane, London. MDCCLX.

(Price Six Shillings and Six Pence, unbound.)

22. John Baskerville of Birmingham printed three editions of The Book of Common Prayer. This is a facsimile of the title page of the first edition in 1760, set in his special large type 'for people who begin to want Spectacles but are ashamed to used them at Church'.

between the thick and thin strokes, the shifting of the second-ary stress (this is caused by the angle at which a pen is held) to a point nearer the vertical, and the widening of most of the small letters.[2] The fount of type Baskerville designed was superior in distinctness and elegance to any previously used.

Baskerville realised from the start of this work that a type face of fine lines and delicate serifs would need clear printing on smooth paper — and a really black ink, instead of the coarser paper and brownish coloured ink then commonly in use. Baskerville poured money into research — employing a Birmingham craftsman to cut most of the thousands of neces-sary punches, establishing his own printing house in the city, discovering the formula for a strong black ink and producing a new type of paper with a glossy finish (it is said that Basker-ville spent £600 before he produced one single letter to his own fastidious satisfaction).

First book in Baskerville

The first book in which the Baskerville type appeared was *The Poems of Virgil*, published in 1757. The great historian Macaulay said that it 'went forth from Birmingham to aston-ish all the librarians of Europe.' This magnificent edition of Virgil was sold at one guinea (£1.05), Matthew Boulton of the Soho Works being one of the first subscribers. Today examples of work from the Baskerville press are very rare.

The Birmingham historian William Hutton, who knew Basker-ville during the latter part of his life, described him as

> a humourist, idle in the extreme but his invention was of the true Birmingham mode — *active*. He could well design, but procured others to execute; wherever Baskerville found merit he caressed it. He was remarkably polite to a stranger, fond of show; a figure rather of the smaller size who delighted to adorn that figure with gold lace . . . if he exhibited a peevish temper we may consider that good nature and intense thinking are not always found together.

At his own request John Baskerville was buried *standing up* under a windmill in the garden of his house. When the canal wharf was under construction at Easy Row in 1821 his body was uncovered, found to be in a good state of preservation and exhibited to the public. This morbid show was stopped by Jonathan Knott, a local bookseller and one-time editor of the *Gazette* in Birmingham. He had Baskerville's body secretly transferred by night to the vaults beneath Christ Church, which then stood in New Street.

Whilst John Baskerville's life and fame as a type founder concentrated attention on Birmingham as a centre of printing art — a reputation maintained ever since by a number of notable city printing houses — books had, in fact, been produced in Birmingham from the early years of the eighteenth century.

A centre of printing art

The earliest book yet discovered with a Birmingham imprint is dated 1717. It was written by James Parkinson, Chief Master of the Free School of Birmingham, and is a classic example of the manner in which the titling of books has changed. Today a few definitive words are sufficient titling, whereas to know what the Birmingham volume of 1717 was about it was necessary to read this title page:

A Loyal Oration, giving a short Account of several Plots, some purely Popish, others mixt; the former contriv'd and Carry'd on by Papists, the latter both by Papists and also Protestants of the High-Church Party, united together against our Church and State: As also of the many Deliverances which Almighty God has Vouchsaf'd to us since the Reformation. Composed by James Parkinson, formerly Fellow of Lincoln College, Oxford, and now Chief Master of the Free School of Birmingham, in Warwickshire, and spoke by his Son, on the 10th day of December, 1716. And now Publish'd at the request of Captain Thetford, Captain Shugborough, and several officers of the Prince's Own Royal Regiment of Welsh Fusileers, and other Loyal Gentlemen. To which is Annex'd by way of Postscript, the Author's Letter to the Reverend Mr. Higgs, Rector of St. Philip's Church in Birmingham, who upon having this Loyal Speech, was so displeas'd and nettl'd with it, and particularly with that Passage in it that relates to bidding Prayers which he constantly uses, that on the Sunday following he could not forbear reviling the Author in his Sermon, calling the Composer thereof a Slanderer and Culminator. Birmingham: Printed and Sold by Matthew Unwins, near St. Martin's Church. 1717.

69

It is likely that this 'Matthew Unwins, near St. Martin's Church', was Birmingham's first printer. Doubtless others soon followed, one of whom was content with the imprint 'H.B. in New Street'.

The early books and pamphlets were poorly printed, unattractive productions. It was a desire to make books beautiful as well as useful that inspired the illustrious John Baskerville to design his elegant type-face and lay the foundations of Birmingham's printing industry. Today, the city's School of Printing is prominent in this field.

Notes

1. From a brochure written by Philip Gaskell and printed at the University Press, Cambridge, on the occasion of Charles Peignot's presentation of the surviving Baskerville type punches to the University of Cambridge in 1953.
2. Ibid.

7. Spectacular Years

Versatility was, and always has been, a characteristic of the city of Birmingham and its craftsmen. Inventors, industrialists and workers moved into Birmingham for two reasons: first, because the skilled labour forces there could turn their hand to anything and, second, because they could get financial backing from prosperous merchants and manufacturers. Moreover, in Birmingham the newcomers could enjoy intelligent and lively company. The era of expansion

Really spectacular growth began around the year 1760 when casting of metals and pattern-makers' moulds improved very considerably. The discovery of mixed metals which could be shaped with stamping machines meant that women, and even quite young children, were employed; Birmingham trades were already using a good deal of machinery before the full impact of the age of steam.

Although the stock bank, opened in 1765 by Taylor and Lloyd, helped industrial investment and therefore the expansion of business, typical small workshops held their place in the town and even to this day have never been entirely abandoned. These small workshops account for Birmingham's reputation as a city of a thousand different trades. The following table charts some of the major events compressed into only thirty years at the end of the eighteenth century:

1769 first canal became operational
1770 Ramsden's screw-cutting lathe
1773 an Assay Office in Birmingham
1774 Dr Priestley discovered oxygen
1775 Watt's steam engine perfected

1776 machine plane invented

1777 William Murdoch discovered gas-lighting

1782 Watt patented the rotative engine

1784 Henry Cort's dry puddling process revolutionised the manufacture of wrought iron

1786 in America a nail-making machine was invented which was to have great impact on the nailing industry of the Midlands, for the patent was secured by Nettlefold of Birmingham. Boulton and Watt installed a steam engine with rotary motion in a cotton factory in Nottinghamshire

1790 first steam rolling-mill in operation

1794 the Birmingham Mint (world's largest independent mint) was founded.

The first historian

One of the keenest observers of this period of the Birmingham industrial scene and its people was the city's first historian, William Hutton. Coming from Derby as a lad of eighteen, Hutton first saw Birmingham in 1741. He fell in love with the city and settled there in 1750. His *History of Birmingham*,[1] published in 1782, remains to this day a fine contemporary portrait of a confident, thriving community that was the fountain-head of industry and inventiveness on which so much of Britain's power and prestige were built during and after the Industrial Revolution.

Hutton's comments on his first visit to Birmingham attest to the highly individual appeal and characteristics of our Second City. Hutton was apprenticed to his uncle, a stocking-maker in Nottingham, but his real interests were in clothes, playing music, women — and books. Some time before he set up as a bookseller in the little Nottinghamshire town of Southwell, Hutton absconded for four days from his uncle's stocking-frame and sought the sights of Birmingham.

'This happy people'

After wandering through Lichfield, where his few possessions were stolen, and Walsall, where he 'thought the people dirty and — particularly the women — very vulgar', he arrived on Handsworth Heath and as he tells us in his book:

had a view of Birmingham. St. Philip's [church] appeared first, uncrowded with houses, untarnished with smoke, and illuminated with a western sun. It appeared in all the pride

72

23. The Victoria and Albert 1967 Christmas silver plate made at the Birmingham Mint. It depicts the Christmas tree at Windsor Castle in 1848. On Christmas Eve 1841 Prince Albert wrote 'my children are full of wonder at the German Christmas tree and its radiant candles.'

of modern architecture. I was charmed with its beauty, and thought it then, as I do now, the credit of the place . . . The outskirts of [other towns] . . . seemed to be composed of wretched dwellings, visibly stamped with dirt and poverty. But the buildings in the exteriors of Birmingham rose in a style of elegance. Thatch, so plentiful in other places, was not to be met with in this.

I was surprised at the place, but more so at the people. They presented a vivacity I had never before beheld. I had been among dreamers, but now I saw men awake. Their very step along the streets showed alacrity. Every man seemed to know what he was about. The town was large, and full of inhabitants and these inhabitants full of industry. The faces of other men seemed tinctured with an idle gloom; but here with a pleasing alertness. Their appearance was strongly marked with the modes of civil life . . . hospitality seemed to claim this happy people for her own.

24. A present day silversmith brazing 'apostle' handles on spoons.

Hutton's words 'full of industry' would have been a motto for Matthew Boulton's Soho Works. The output was increasing all the time and this sheer volume of manufacture created its own problems. Indeed, it was such problems which convinced Matthew Boulton to link up with James Watt to develop the steam engine. By the time Boulton and Watt formed their partnership, John Fothergill — the super-salesman for Soho — had retired from the scene, exhausted by the incessant financial anxieties resulting from Boulton's many enthusiasms.

Other, more academic personalities were to play an important role in furthering Boulton's ambitions. These influential men included Dr John Roebuck (see also Chapter 5); another physician, Dr William Small, who took out patents for improved clock movements and was instrumental in introducing James Watt to Matthew Boulton; Dr Erasmus Darwin FRS (grandfather of Charles Darwin, author of *The Origin of Species*), a distinguished philosopher, scientist and physician from whom Matthew Boulton gained the greater part of the scientific education denied him in his youth; Samuel Garbett, agitator-in-chief for the pottery king Josiah Wedgwood's campaign for canals in Birmingham; and another canal promoter named John Whitehurst, a Derby clock- and instrument-maker.

These six learned gentlemen were good friends sharing interests in industrial progress as well as sponsoring inland waterways. All were founder members of the famous Lunar Society of Birmingham (see next chapter) to which Dr Small, a gentle and lovable Scotsman 'happily gifted in communicating the most useful branches of science', acted as chief convener.

Note

1. A facsimile of Hutton's second edition of 1783 was published in 1976 by EP Publishing Ltd, Wakefield.

8. The Lunar Society

A scientific forum

With many brilliant scientists, inventors and engineers working and living in and around eighteenth-century Birmingham it followed quite naturally that an élite should meet socially for the professional sharing of knowledge. For some forty years such a group met regularly in the town and in 1776 they formed the Lunar Society. It became, with the exception of the Royal Society in London, the most famous English scientific society of the seventeenth and eighteenth centuries and was so named because meetings were planned to coincide with times of the full moon in order that out-of-town members could 'have the benefit of its light in returning home'.

The Society had few set rules and kept no records of its proceedings. The members met by turns at each other's houses, there to exchange news not only on scientific matters but also on literature and art. One of the members was Matthew Boulton (see Chapter 4) whose home was referred to as 'l'hôtel de l'amitie sur Handsworth Heath'.

The distinguished people who attended the first Lunar Society meeting included:

Matthew Boulton	Capt. James Keir
Dr Erasmus Darwin	James Watt
Dr William Small	Dr William Withering
John Whitehurst	Dr Joseph Priestley
Josiah Wedgwood	Samuel Galton jun.
Richard Lovell Edgeworth	Dr Jonathan Stokes
Thomas Day	The Rev. Robert A. Johnson

Besides Boulton, who delighted in entertaining the society in the grand manner at his house, another who enjoyed acting host was Samuel Galton, a Quaker and wealthy industrialist. Galton shared the members' passion for inventions and experiments (it was his butler who referred to Lunar Society members as 'the lunatics').

The great
Dr Priestley

The greatest scientist among them was chemist and clergyman Dr Joseph Priestley — a man, it was said, 'no less distinguished by social and christian virtues than scientific and literary attainments'. Priestley, in dedicating his book, *Experiments on the Generation of Air from Water*, to the Lunar Society, wrote:

> There are few things that I more regret in consequence of my removal from Birmingham than the loss of your society. It both encouraged and enlightened me; so that what I did there of a philosophical kind ought in justice to be attributed almost as much to you as myself. From our cheerful meetings I have never absented myself voluntarily, and from my pleasing recollection they will never be absent.

Dr Priestley is now regarded as 'the father of modern chemistry'. He arrived in Birmingham to take up his appointment as Minister to the Unitarian Congregation; this was said to be the most intellectually vigorous congregation in the country, radical in politics, cultivated in the arts and sciences, and deeply involved in the civic life of the city.

A French visitor wrote of Priestley: 'he employs his time in a variety of studies. History, moral philosophy, and religion, occupy his attention by turns... at his side an educated wife, a lovely daughter, and in a charming residence where everything bespoke industry, peace and happiness.'[1]

Priestley, who belonged to the old Dissenting tradition, became pastor of the Old Meeting House which the Dissenters of Birmingham had built for themselves after the 1689 Act of Tolerance was passed. This Act allowed Protestant Dissenters from the Established Church to worship God according to their own conscience.

Dr Priestley fearlessly proclaimed his religious and political convictions. Some considered him over-zealous, instancing his introduction of controversial theology into Birmingham Library. Dr Priestley's sympathy with the French Revolution added to growing opposition in the town and led up to the Birmingham riots of 1791. Birmingham, at this time, still provided a rural setting but, alas, the peace of Priestley's home was totally shattered when a rioting mob burnt the doctor's house, books, manuscripts and instruments. Dr Priestley and his family were fortunate in escaping with their lives but prejudice followed this gentle philosopher to London and soon afterwards he left Britain for Pennsylvania, where he died in 1804. The following description of part of the Priestley riots is given in *A Short History of Birmingham* by J. Ernest Jones (see also picture on p. 29).

The New Meeting House was broken open without ceremony, the pews, cushions, books and pulpit were dashed to pieces and in half an hour the whole was ablaze, while the savage multitude rejoiced at the view. Then the Old Meeting House was destroyed, after which the mob undertook a march of more than a mile to the house of Dr. Priestley [at Fair Hill, Sparkhill] which was plundered and burnt without mercy, the doctor and his family barely escaping with their lives.

All Dr Priestley's scientific apparatus, his unpublished manuscripts and his rare and valuable library were lost in these riots which lasted almost a week and which local magistrates were unable to check. The riots caused £50,000 worth of damage and much distress. As the days went by the drunken mobs attacked many of the big houses in or near the town. Among the houses set fire to were those of John Taylor, a leading button manufacturer; William Hutton, bookseller and local historian; and that of John Baskerville, the printer.

With the exception of Dr Priestley, all the members of the Lunar Society were very free-thinking in their attitude to religion. And all but one of them became Fellows of the Royal Society. It was these men who led the country into the great era of steam power and they stand forth as the initiators of the research and development which helped to solve the practical problems of the quickening Industrial Revolution.

Scientists from abroad

77

25. Erasmus Darwin — a 1770 portrait in oils by Joseph Wright of Derby (the same artist painted 'The Forge' reproduced on the jacket of this book)

Although Lunar Society meetings were exclusive and private gatherings, the group benefited from contacts with distinguished men of science both at home and abroad. The most eminent scientists of the day, such as naturalist and explorer Sir Joseph Banks and Sir William Herschel, the German musician and astronomer, occasionally attended as guests.

The Lunar Society's link with Scotland was a particularly strong one. At the time, Edinburgh was famous as the great provincial centre of learning — free from the domination of the Church of England which blinkered Oxford and Cambridge Universities, for both still excluded all dissenters and Roman Catholics.

Contribution of medical men

Among the early Lunar Society members were three Scotsmen and three medical men trained at Edinburgh. Dr Small, a Scottish minister's son, was one of the Lunar Society's medical members. He had been appointed Professor of Natural Philosophy in the University of Williamsburg, Virginia, but as the climate did not suit his health, he returned to Britain and settled in Birmingham, commencing practice as a physician at No. 9 Temple Row, where he quickly acquired eminence. It was Dr Small, a man of singular amiability of character, who brought Boulton and Watt together. He was in

78

26. An engraving of James Keir (in the possession of the Royal Society). Both men were eminent scientists and members of the Lunar Society.

fact, the connecting link between members of the Lunar Society with all their differing specialities and knowledge.

Dr Small's death in 1775, when only 41, was a serious blow to the Society. It came as he was about to be invited into the partnership at Soho, and Boulton felt the loss of his friend very keenly. Captain James Keir, another founder member of the Lunar Society, spoke of Dr Small as one 'who, to the most extensive, various and accurate knowledge in the sciences, in literature and in life, joined engaging manners, a most exact conduct, a liberality of sentiment and enlightened humanity'.

Of the other medical members the most dominating and the most versatile was Dr Erasmus Darwin from Lichfield. Apart from being an able and generous physician, beloved by his patients, Darwin's versatility was evidenced in his published works relating to such diverse subjects as the classification of vegetables and flowers, natural history, a book called *A Plan for the Conduct of Female Education in Boarding Schools*, and poetry – including a long poem called 'The Botanic Garden', which remains unique as the only best-selling English poem on a scientific subject.

Physician and poet

79

Darwin delighted in the academic brilliance of the Lunar Society. Sometimes, when too busy to attend, the host would receive a letter like this:

> Dear Boulton,
>
> I am sorry the infernal divinities who visit mankind with diseases . . . should have prevented me seeing all you great men at Soho to-day. Lord! what inventions, what wit, what rhetoric, metaphysical, mechanical and pyrotechnical, will be on the wing, bandied like a shuttlecock from one to another of your troup of philosophers! while poor I, I by my self I, imprison'd in a post-chaise, am joggl'd, and jostl'd and bump'd, and bruised along the King's highroad to make war upon a pox or a fever . . .[2]

Darwin's activity was astonishing. Medicine, literature, scientific study and mechanical invention . . . and about 1777 he bought 'a little wild, umbrageous valley, a mile from Lichfield, irriguous from various springs, and swampy from their plentitude'.[3] Here he exercised his mechanical and botanical skills to transform eight acres of swamp into a pleasure garden and herboretum, damming the streams to make lakes, and erecting flower-lined walks among the drained marshes.

Darwin's interest in botany was shared by a fellow member of the Lunar Society, Dr William Withering — a co-founder, with Dr John Ash, of Birmingham General Hospital. Dr Withering lived at Edgbaston Hall and is remembered not only for his classification of botanical specimens but also for making generally known the value of the foxglove drug digitalis in treating heart disease. He published his observations in *An Account of the Foxglove and some of its Medical Uses*, produced in Birmingham in 1785. When Dr Withering died in 1799 a foxglove was carved on his tombstone in Edgbaston Old Church.

Their own factories

A feature of the Lunar Society was the way in which friends — Boulton, Watt, Wedgwood, Priestley, Darwin, Keir — was each a friend of all the others, and remained so. Reading in turn biographies of each, the others regularly appear. The Society's strength undoubtedly lay in the fact that most of its members had practical experience in manufacturing and

80

all were interested in the problems it posed. In no small measure it was these men who, by sharing their knowledge and expertise, led Birmingham to become the city of 'engineers to the world'.

Four of the Lunar Society members were running their own factories: Matthew Boulton, manufacturing metal articles at Soho; Captain James Keir owned an alkali works at Tipton (James Watt described him as 'a mighty chemist before the Lord and a very agreeable man'[4]); Josiah Wedgwood had pottery works at Etruria, in Staffordshire; and Samuel Galton specialised in gun-making (to the annoyance of his co-religionists).

The Lunar Society's contribution to the advancement of industrial science largely came by way of the exchange of ideas and knowledge — over a pleasant midday dinner. This process of 'cross-fertilisation' led, for example, to discussions between Josiah Wedgwood and Darwin over the establishment of the Grand Trunk Canal which was to run through Wedgwood's new works at Etruria. Dr Priestley was able to meet Wedgwood's request for a satisfactory mortar to use in ceramics (this mortar was later used in the manufacture of scientific apparatus throughout the land).

Exchange of ideas

Darwin and Watt were able to provide Wedgwood with sound advice and valuable experimental material, thus helping Wedgwood to produce as a sideline the first earthenware drain-pipes and water-pipes. The production of these greatly improved sanitation and public health and became one of the country's big industries. More widely recognised as a major contribution to public health is Wedgwood's 'Queensware'. Made of a relatively cheap and durable paste, this tableware replaced utensils made from wood, tin or pewter and was considerably easier to keep clean.

The shrewd and popular chemist Captain James Keir seems to have acted most often as chairman of the Society gatherings. He went to live at West Bromwich about 1768 and in the late 1770s founded the Tipton alkali works — second only to Matthew Boulton's Soho Works as a marvel of technology and marking the birth of today's chemical industry.

Keir, born in Edinburgh in 1735, trained as a doctor and was a close friend of Erasmus Darwin. Like the historian Hutton before him, he visited — and liked — Birmingham, decided to settle there and began an industrial career as a glass-maker at nearby Stourbridge. Keir had, in turn, been a doctor, soldier, manufacturer, chemist and, finally, philosopher. One of the patents he took out was for 'a compound metal capable of being forged when red hot or when cold, more fit for the making of bolts, nails and sheathing for ships than any metal heretofore used or supplied for those purposes'.

Richard Lovell Edgeworth, listed earlier as among those who attended the first meeting of the Lunar Society, made notable contributions to education. Remarkable for his powers or mechanical invention, Edgeworth was a fervent disciple of Jean Rousseau, the eighteenth-century French writer and philosopher whose book *Emile* expounded a new system of education based on natural development and the power of example. Edgeworth, in co-operation with his daughter Maria (one of his 22 children by four wives) published *Practical Education* in 1798. This book not only endorsed the educational ideas of Dr Priestley but also formed the basis of later progressive educational methods.

Among the important emancipating factors which would improve conditions in the future were increasing trade and better communications with other parts of the country, and in this respect the Lunar Society can claim some credit, since its members included some very influential promoters of canals. If the vast network of waterways had not been opened up, the Industrial Revolution would not have been possible in the form we know it.

Notes

1. B. Faujas-Saint-Fond, in *Voyages en Angleterre, en Ecosse, et Aux Iles Hebrides* (Paris, 1797).
2. H. Carrington Boulton, *Scientific Correspondence of Joseph Priestley* (New York, 1892); E. Robinson (ed.), *Annals of Science* (London, 1953).
3. Anna Seward, *Memoirs of the Life of Dr Darwin* (London, 1804).
4. 'Watt on Keir', *University of Birmingham Historical Journal*, p. 52.

9. Hidden World of Canals

Canals are a fascinating feature of Birmingham and there are more miles of these silent highways in the city than in Venice.[1] These canals are part of a strange and hidden world — almost unknown even to the city's inhabitants and very rarely seen by visitors. Admittedly, there is, in places, a Stygian gloom about the scene — but this in itself acts as a powerful reminder of the industrial situation before the railways came and of the rugged men and women who lived out their lives carrying coal and other essential cargoes of the Industrial Revolution in canal narrow boats. The hidden canal scene in the heart of Birmingham is as emotionally moving as, and reminiscent of, a Lowry painting of the industrial North with all its poignancy and reflective drama.

More canals than Venice

By no means as colourful as it used to be before builders' demolition squads moved in, Gas Street canal basin is still characteristic of the canal's part in Birmingham life. Turn off the noisy, busy Broad Street and down the narrow, high-walled Gas Street and one finds a gap in the wall and some steps leading down to the water. It is a place apart, a place of 'atmosphere'. On one side of the basin, where the gaily pain-ted narrow boats used to unload their cargo, is an attractive cobbled path, with a few old boat folk still about and a few of the original eighteenth-century cottages — one now a booking-office for the Birmingham canal hire boats. On the other side — nothing now but an ugly open space awaiting the building of a new office block.

This world has much to offer that is interesting in compari-son with the bland sophistication of the city centre . . . such place names as Spoon Lane and Pudding Green,

27. Working narrow boats in Gas Street basin, 1910.

83

Wednesbury Oak, Tipton and Bumbledown, Oozells Street Loop and Brasshouse Bridge deserve their own hymns of praise . . . the canal route winds its way through the strange, rather quirky places such names would lead you to expect . . . and even the 20th century had added its own rather spectacular visual effects to the canals. The motorways, such a feature of the Birmingham scene, look more interesting when seen from underneath. The M.5, for example, crosses the canal on tall stilts like a huge colonnade, but for those who want a real motorway wonderland I recommend a trip down the Birmingham and Fazeley canal, where it slides through a forest of columns that support the tangle of roads that make up Spaghetti Junction.[2]

There were no canals in England before the mid-eighteenth century. Cargo vessels used rivers where navigation was possible and horse-drawn covered wagons carried goods like coal and food to the small towns. As with all rivers, the Severn and the Trent varied in depth and strength of current at different times of the year. Weirs were constructed to ease navigation and provide water power for mills on the river banks.

The canal frenzy

To straighten out bends in the rivers, the first 'cut' was constructed in 1759. Two parts of the Sankey Brook, on the River Mersey, were then joined by a canal. It proved a prosperous venture for all concerned and led to further plans to link waterways and finally to the 'canal frenzy'.

A lot of people, however, did not want canals. Farmers, for example, were afraid they would cut through their arable fields. Millers using water power were worried that their water power would be drained away — a most important consideration since as many as 48 water mills were working on Birmingham rivers in the early eighteenth century. On the other hand, construction of canals was entirely beneficial to the new professionals — lawyers, bank managers, architects and engineers among them. It brought them together in a joint enterprise and linked them up with the landed gentry through whose estates the canals were to pass. This fusion of classes was an asset to all concerned, particularly where big landowners also had rich deposits of minerals — such as coal and ironstone. Thus the development of canals, and the immense industrial growth they helped make possible before the railway age, was exploited by those progressive members of the aristocracy who saw in the canal frenzy a profit for themselves. Even at this stage in political history, the same private enterprise would probably have been impossible in other countries, where the King or the state itself stood to benefit (rather than individual landowners) from the exploitation of mineral deposits.

Enthusiasm soon replaced the early opposition and canal construction proceeded apace. Irish labourers did most of the building work and these rough and tough canal navigators (or 'navvies') were confined to special enclosures on the building sites in order to protect the local population. These men slowly dug their way across the Midlands, finishing on the high plateau on which Birmingham stands.

The first moves to promote a canal company in Birmingham were made by the Lunar Society (see previous chapter). An Act of 1761 permitted 'a cut in connection with Birmingham'

28. The Birmingham Canal Navigation Company offices and Victorian gas-lamps in Paradise Street shortly before demolition around 1913.

and the first section linked the city with Staffordshire coal-fields. It was opened in 1769. The following year this was extended to Wolverhampton, where it joined the Stafford-shire-Worcestershire canal to the River Severn — thus giving Birmingham an efficient waterway to Bristol and other ports. By 1790, when the Grand Union Canal was opened, Birming-ham was also linked with London.

Initial planning of the Birmingham and Wolverhampton canal, financed by the Birmingham Canal Navigation Company, was done by the engineer James Brindley, famed for his work with the Duke of Bridgewater in constructing classic early canals in the mid-eighteenth century. But the great Brindley, who began life as a Derbyshire wheelwright's apprentice, did not live to see the £70,000 Birmingham project finished. His work was taken up by John Smeaton (engineer of the Forth and Clyde Canal) and Thomas Telford, the engineering genius who — besides his many great road works — built the Menai Strait suspension bridge on the Holyhead road across Angle-sey.

On the construction of the Birmingham and Wolverhampton canal Hutton, the local historian, says,

> the managers, not being able to find patience to worm round the hill at Smethwick, or cut through it, wisely travelled over it by the help of twelve locks — with six they mount the summit, and with six more descend to the former level; forgetting the great waste of water, and the small supply from the rivulets, in climbing this curious ladder of twelve liquid steps.

Telford's
improvements

The inconvenience of navigating these twelve locks in order to reach the 460-foot summit was a source of continued complaint, and it was Telford who removed them by cutting through the hills to a perpendicular depth of more than 70 feet.[3] Telford, who described the original plans as 'a crooked ditch', straightened and shortened the route from 22 to 14 miles. The completed canal was described by Hutton as being 'unsurpassed in stupendous magnificence by any similar work in the world'.

Canals proved as great an industrial breakthrough as did the invention of an efficient steam engine. This opening up of communications enabled Birmingham to become a leading industrial and business centre not only for the United Kingdom, but also for Europe and America. In the town canal banks became so thick with workshops that by 1811 no less than 124 works and wharfs crowded the two miles of canal between Bordsley and Aston — some of them in converted former water-mills. Merchants and factors made their headquarters in Birmingham, providing the finance, raw materials and marketing which inspired Birmingham's remarkable climb to fame and fortune.

The new canal age transformed eighteenth-century Birmingham into an inland port and the hub of a national system of waterways. By bringing south Staffordshire and other coalfields within easy reach, the price of coal was halved. This became a prime factor in promoting rapid industrial expansion.

The *Gazette* newspaper in Birmingham reported extensively on all canal developments. It recorded how, when the parliamentary Bill for making the Birmingham to Wolverhampton canal received royal assent on 26 July 1768, the 'agreeable news reached Birmingham and the bells were set to ringing, which were continued the whole day'.

Link with Wolverhampton

Canal-opening ceremonies were often grand occasions, the company directors embarking on barges decorated with flags. Bands played the national anthem and in certain areas Army guns were fired in salute. The first boatload of Black Country coal was brought to Birmingham by canal on 7 November 1769, and a few days beforehand the *Gazette* had this to say:

> It is with Pleasure we congratulate the Public on the probability of Coal being brought by Water near this Town in a few Days; and that the Canal Company have not only resolved to sell the same this Winter at their Wharf for Fourpence Half-penny per Hundred, long weight of 120 lbs., but to fix the Price of their Delivery in every Street thereof: and in order for the better accomodation of the Poor, they have determined to establish Coal-Yards in different parts of the Town as soon as possible, where it will be sold in Quantities as small as Half-Hundreds, no less.

An office for the canal company's business was built at the western end of Paradise Street (then called Paradise Row), and it was from the steps of this office that John Wesley preached during some of his many visits to Birmingham.

For over sixty years the network of canals in and around Birmingham grew more and more complex, complete with wharfs and warehouses. The products of almost every major firm in the country were carried on canals. Birmingham was the centre of the navigation network as it was eventually to become the hub of the nation's road transport system.

Two hundred years of service

Today, a large area of the West Midlands is dominated by a Birmingham-Black Country conurbation with a population of over three million people. The canals are still there, but their use as trading arteries was doomed with the coming of the railways in the nineteenth century. Nevertheless, an outstanding fact about the canal network of Birmingham and the Midlands is that it has proved so durable. Canals like the Trent and Mersey, Staffordshire and Worcester, Coventry and Oxford carried considerable traffic for nearly two hundred years — that is to say, far longer than any significant railway line or most turnpike roads.

In 1830 the Liverpool and Manchester Railway opened, and the railway boom began. Everywhere, canal companies had to cut their rates to compete — but in vain. Suddenly no one wanted the canals any more and investors rushed to switch their money into railways. (The achievement of linking Birmingham with London by rail is described in Chapter 11.)

Unsuccessful attempts were made at this time to get some form of rail-canal integration. For instance, the Shropshire Union was acquired by the London and North Western Railway and leased on the understanding that long-haul traffic was for rail and the canal-owners could develop specialised trades within its local system. The same principles were applied to the development of the Birmingham Canal Navigations, also with the LNWR as masters.

As a postscript to the canal story, it was the late L.T.C. Rolt who wrote in his much-loved book *Narrow Boat* about the canals and rivers of England, for so long threatened by

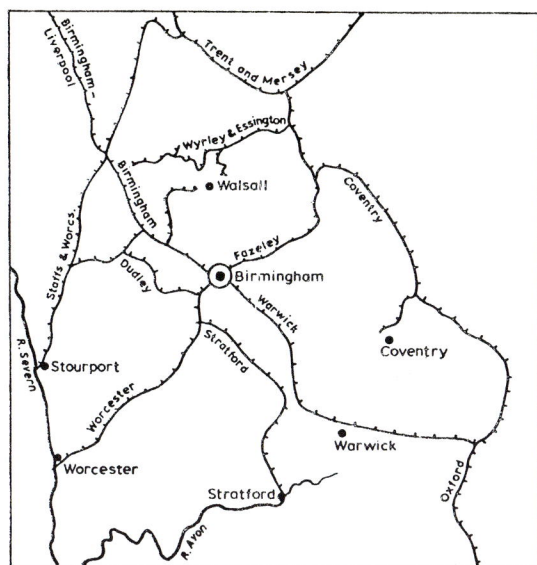

29. The canal network around and into Birmingham.

30. Today the canals are increasingly used for leisure pursuits. This was the scene near Gas Street basin in 1969 at the National Waterways Association rally.

91

neglect, maltreatment and pollution: 'our waterways are at once a transport system, a source of water supply and land drainage, a sporting amenity as well as a characteristic feature of our countryside.' Rolt, in 1947, was right in welcoming — partly as a result of his book — the setting up of the Inland Waterways Association to safeguard this part of our heritage. Since then much good restoration work has been done — and much still remains to be done.

Notes

1. Walter Showell's *Dictionary of Birmingham* (1885), republished by EP Publishing, Wakefield, in 1969, gives a figure of 130 miles — or 250 miles if Black Country canals are added in.

2. Anthony Barton writing in *Back Door Britain*, an account of a 1,000-mile canal journey (London, Andre Deutsch, 1977).

3. Robert K. Dent, *Old and New Birmingham* (first published 1878-80), republished by EP Publishing, Wakefield, 1972. Birmingham is situated on a high plateau and this caused some difficulties. In constructing the first 'crooked ditch', keeping the cost down was more important than time — hence many locks. Also, canals, like rivers, have to be filled from somewhere — hence the construction of reservoirs at frequent intervals.

10. Guns and Jewellery

The cheapness of coal brought into Birmingham by canal was instrumental not only in the rise of the British coal industry itself, and the expansion of industry generally, but was also a prime factor in enabling Birmingham to supersede London as the centre of gun-making. By the middle of the seventeenth century coal had become indispensable for forging the metal parts of guns and early London gunsmiths were hard hit whenever coal supplies were held up. Birmingham also scored in having an unrivalled knowledge of metal-working.

How cheap coal helped

During the seventeenth century a flintlock gun was introduced into Britain from Germany, where the mechanism had been patented by Heinrich Thielmans as early as 1598. In Germany it was known as the *Donner-busch*, i.e. thunder-gun, and when it came to Birmingham the local craftsmen eagerly took up its manufacture — calling it the blunderbuss. It soon became in general use on most coaches for protection against highwaymen.

The earliest official record of the Birmingham gun trade is, significantly, a government contract. On 10 January 1689 the Office of the Ordnance wrote to Sir Richard Newdigate, of Arbury in Warwickshire, saying that two spring-lock muskets were being sent and asking that they should be shown to the Birmingham workmen: the Board would be glad to know whether these local craftsmen could copy the muskets, whether enough could be made in Birmingham to warrant sending an officer from London to prove the guns (by the Tower proof), and what the price of the muskets would be.

Two hundred muskets a month

On 26 March 1692 a trial order was given to Birmingham, followed soon after by a contract for a year's supply of arms at the rate of 200 muskets a month. The weapons were for use in the wars against Louis XIV of France. Two years later five Birmingham gunsmiths were named in a further government contract for 2,400 muskets priced at 17 shillings each. The gunsmiths were William Bourne, Thomas Moore, John West, Richard Weston and Jacob Austin, and the guns were to be proofed in Birmingham, not London.

From the city's early success in the gun trade it became the practice of governments in wartime to look to Birmingham as the main source not only of guns but other types of war material, including bayonets and ammunition. In the latter phases of the Napoleonic Wars, between 1804 and 1815, Birmingham made some three million gun barrels and a similar quantity of gun-locks for the government — this was two-thirds of the total requirements of the Army and Navy and a greater output than that of the ten state arsenals of France.[1] The city also made the swords used by the Duke of Wellington's army in the Battle of Waterloo. A Birmingham gun-lock known as Brown Bess was used on the standard British military flintlock musket by the mid-eighteenth century.

Jealousy
in London

The development of the gun trade in Birmingham, as with other great achievements of our Second City, did not come easily. Its early, struggling days were full of jealousy and intrigue between Birmingham and London. The official letter of 1689 already referred to upset the London gun-makers and they aired their grievances in Parliament. In his book published in 1938, Professor Court wrote, 'Nor can the lofty attitude of the Midland men have improved relations in the next few years, if their styling themselves the Company of Gunmakers in Birmingham, in a letter to Sir Richard Newdigate, can be taken as at all typical.'[2]

There was no legal foundation for such a company and the claim naturally angered the well established and properly constituted London gun-makers' organisation. Nearly twenty years later a petition from the Birmingham craftsmen reached Parliament, complaining of the London men making life difficult for provincial competitors. Be that as it may, the Birmingham gun-makers grew in strength and became a striking example of the importance of new industries which were setting up in Birmingham and exporting abroad towards the end of the eighteenth century.

City helped by gun trade

The gun trade was vital to Birmingham at the time when the wars in France had led to trade depression. There was much suffering, with many people out of work and hungry, yet the city was more fortunate than many other manufacturing towns thanks to both the gun trade and the great variety of goods made in the small workshops.

Birmingham had a natural advantage over London in being situated very near to the source of iron, steel and coal. Old horseshoes, nails and stubs were often added to improve the quality of gun-metal. When various metals were hammered together into one block the result was called the 'bloom', which came out as a riband of metal several yards long from which a gun-barrel was skilfully fashioned by eye, using cast shadows to help keep the lines straight. Some of Birmingham's sword-makers turned successfully to gun-making, and from an annual production of 400 guns in 1708 the output eventually grew to over 150,000 guns a year. Many of these guns were exported to America, the East Indies and Africa. Tribesmen in Africa were bribed with flint muskets, many of which had reached Africa in the holds of ships carrying missionaries eager to convert the natives to Christianity. Other guns from Birmingham were exchanged for furs in North America, and some — mostly muzzle-loading weapons using a ramrod to push home the charge of gunpowder — also went to the West Indies and South America.

Days of the one-man shop

A characteristic of the early Birmingham gun trade — as, indeed, of the city's famous 'jewellery quarter' (see later this chapter) - was the manner in which so many different, highly skilled craftsmen exercised their skills in small, congested workshops. In each workshop there were two groups, each with clearly defined (and often strangely named) tasks. The first group included stock-makers, barrel-welders, borers, grinders, filers and breechers; rib-makers, breech-forgers and stampers; lock-forgers, machiners and filers; furniture forgers, casters and filers; rod forgers, grinders, polishers and finishers; bayonet-forgers, socket and ring stampers, hardeners and filers; band forgers, stampers, machiners, filers and pin-makers; sight-stampers; trigger boxes and oddwork makers. The second group in a workshop — the 'setters-up' — included machiners, jiggers, stockers, percussioners, screwers, strippers, barrel-borers and riflers, sighters, smoothers, makers-off, polishers, engravers, browners and lock-freers.

Names that
made history

The names of some of the skilled Birmingham master gun-smiths have passed into military, sporting and even legal history. Among them was John Waters who, in the late eighteenth century, made very fine pistols — as well as blunderbusses — examples of which can be seen in the Birmingham Science Museum.

John Waters figured in a dispute which aroused great contro-versy in the town. In 1781 he patented a form of spring bayonet on his guns but was then petitioned against by a William Grice who claimed that Waters had stolen his inven-tion of five years previously. This was followed by another Birmingham gunsmith, Thomas Gill, also claiming that the invention was his. The dispute was somehow settled and the spring bayonet taken up and improved on by gunsmiths everywhere.

T. Pocock was another distinguished gunsmith in the late eighteenth century. He won fame for his handsome flintlock pistols with silver-wire inlaid butts and beautiful engraving. Later, in the nineteenth century, came such names as that of William Tranter, maker of cartridge revolvers and who, in 1853, patented the Tranter double-trigger action and, fifteen years later, the rim-fire revolver.

The famous
Proof House

Before Belgium became a big exporter of guns to Britain in the 1880s, and the Royal Ordnance Factory was established at Enfield near London, Birmingham supplied nearly every firearm sold in Britain or exported from the country. Guns were tested at the Birmingham Proof House in Banbury Street, a building (just visible from the London-Birmingham train window) designed in 1813 by John Horton. The Birmingham gun-barrel proof mark of a crown over crossed sceptres is known the world over. Above the entrance to the Proof House is an inscription 'established for the public safety' and the surrounding splendidly coloured emblems are the work of

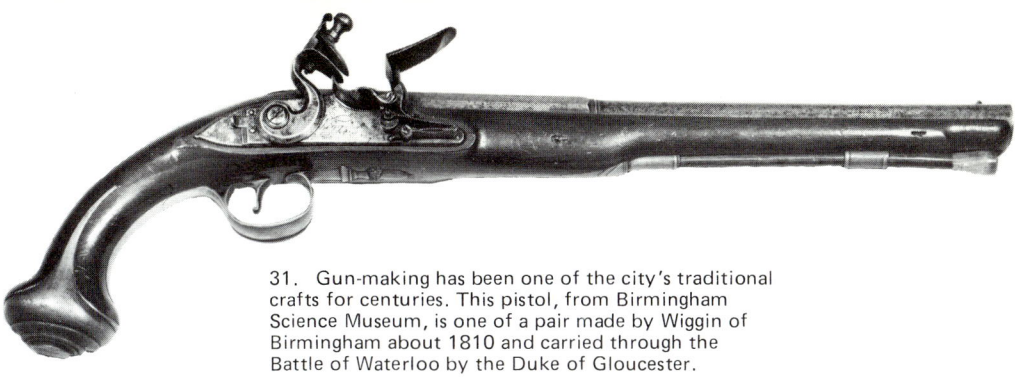

31. Gun-making has been one of the city's traditional crafts for centuries. This pistol, from Birmingham Science Museum, is one of a pair made by Wiggin of Birmingham about 1810 and carried through the Battle of Waterloo by the Duke of Gloucester.

Peter Hollins, sculptor son of William Hollins, a local architect. It was William Hollins who was invited to the Court of Catherine of Russia to submit plans for the Royal Mint in St Petersburg (now Leningrad).

In 1861 the Birmingham Small Arms factory was built at Smallheath. It extended over 25 acres of land and developed into the largest private arms establishment in Europe. However, it was not BSA but the already mentioned small master gunsmiths, closely packed into the area behind the Cathedral of St Chad, who first made Birmingham world-famous for guns. Apart from the guns which went to Africa, the East and West Indies, and South America, hundreds of thousands of hand-made Birmingham guns were exported to America at the time of the Civil War 1861-5; the guns used in the Franco-German war of the 1870s were almost all Birmingham-made; and a batch of Birmingham guns was smuggled into South Africa for use in the Jameson Raid of 1895, which precipitated the Boer War (some of these guns left Birmingham secreted in packing cases designed to resemble grand pianos!).[3]

Export of armaments

The contribution, in terms of armaments, of the BSA factories in the world wars of 1914-18 and 1939-45 was enormous. In the first of these wars the bulk of the rifles and armaments, as well as engines for the first tanks, came from the Birmingham factories. In the Second World War, after the evacuation of Dunkirk, BSA controlled 67 factories, employed 28,000 workers and provided more than half the entire small arms supplied to Britain's fighting men.

The years following the last war brought startling changes in the life-style of cities throughout the land, not least to Birmingham. In many trades the small, one-man business

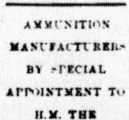

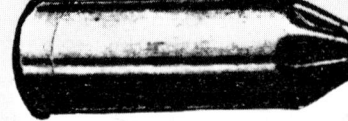
32. Ammunition of all kinds, in peace and war, poured out of Birmingham factories. Kynoch (an early catalogue cover is shown here) and Eley are names known to sportsmen the world over.

began to disappear and this has been true of the city's traditional gun trade — the distinctive gunsmiths' quarter has now almost vanished. Their locality, along with many other parts of the old 'Brum', was redeveloped. Today, only a few small gunsmiths are left — providing top-quality hand-made guns for sportsmen.

A large group of skilled masters running small individual workshops was characteristic of the gun trade and equally so of jewellery and glass-making, two other trades introduced into Birmingham in the late eighteenth and early nineteenth centuries. But the jewellers were far fewer in number in those early days, there being — apart from some purely one-man concerns — not quite a dozen sizeable jewellery firms in the town.

A start in jewellery

Again, like the gun trade, the city's reputation for fine jewellery was not easily won. There was a time when buyers were often sceptical of the quality of Birmingham-made jewellery. This gave rise to the saying, 'give a Birmingham man a guinea and a copper kettle and he'll make you a hundred pounds worth of jewellery!'

Prior to the middle of the eighteenth century the sweepings from goldsmiths' and silversmiths' workshops were swept out into the streets. It was thought that sweepings to the value of some thousands of pounds were buried beneath some of the streets. This piece of folklore led to the description of city thoroughfares being 'literally paved with gold and silver'. However, around the year 1758 a Birmingham 'gold dustman' — in other words a sweeper-up — discovered the secret of making a good living from the waste sweepings by the process of refining. This is done by chemically removing impurities and was an art which, for many years, was practised only in Birmingham.

Today, and indeed for many years past, Birmingham jewellers are leaders in matters of taste and design. The city has its own Assay Office (for the analysis of metals), established in 1773. The anchor symbol of the Birmingham Assay Office is, like the Proof House markings on guns tested in Birmingham, famous the world over. A considerable quantity of civic regalia, mayoral chains and similar items are produced in the city.

33. Jewellery in the medieval style made by J. Hardman of Birmingham for the designer Pugin and shown at the Great Exhibition at the Crystal Palace in 1851.

34. Workshops in the jewellery quarter.

Although eleven 'glass-pinchers'[4] are named in a Birmingham directory of 1780, in this final quarter of the eighteenth century Birmingham and the rest of the Midlands had largely been supplied with glass — particularly tableware — from the renowned glass-making centre of Stourbridge, in the neighbouring county of Worcestershire. The man who brought the art to Birmingham was Isaac Hawker who, in 1785, built a small works in Edgbaston Street.

This 'new' trade of the period was closely connected with the Birmingham jewellery-makers, at the start turning out glass beads and bits for the toy trade. Here again it was Birmingham's good fortune that the fireclay needed for glasshouse-pots (in which the basic materials for glass are fused) was available from the coalfields of the neighbouring Black Country. The special type of sand required for glass-making was obtained from King's Lynn in Norfolk and delivered to Birmingham by river and canal.

The industry prospered. More glass-houses were opened and Isaac Hawker's son later built the first large works, on Birmingham Heath. Another Birmingham name prominent in the mid-nineteenth-century history of glass-making is that of James Stevens, then of Camden Street in the city. Stevens worked on an American invention, introduced in 1832, for the pressing of glass. This is a technique, adaptable to mechanical methods, in which molten glass is pressed into required shapes in a mould as distinct from the older glass-blowing process.

Credit for early glass-pressing thus goes to Birmingham. None of the samples of early Venetian glass show any pressing, although moulding was of the highest perfection. Similarly, it was in Birmingham that another special process — now lost — of painting or staining on glass was brought to perfection by Francis Eginton, who joined the Soho Works in 1784. Eginton supplied windows for St George's Chapel, Windsor; Lichfield and Salisbury Cathedrals; St Paul's, Birmingham; and Aston Church.

In the nineteenth century Birmingham glass-makers adopted a policy of using more expensive methods than were common elsewhere (in Newcastle for example) and Birmingham became the source of the very best glass obtainable anywhere. By 1866 there were seventeen large glass furnaces in Birmingham. In the early 1880s some factories — such as Jones, Smart & Co. at Aston Hill — installed that wonder of the Victorian age, gas lighting, and were described as being 'light as day'. Coal-gas lighting had first been used in 1792 by the Scottish engineer William Murdoch to light his own house. Six years later it was installed at Birmingham's renowned Soho Foundry and all the gas lamps were lit at the factory for the 1802 Peace of Amiens celebrations 'to the delight [reported the Birmingham *Gazette*] and astonishment of the city's inhabitants'.

The large glass-making concerns included those of the Chance Brothers at Smethwick, just outside Birmingham, and F. & C. Osler. For the glazing of the Crystal Palace at the Great Exhibition of 1851 the Chance firm (and it was they who first introduced sheet glass into England about 1832) made nearly a million square feet of glass. The Chance Brothers also made flint glass for optical purposes (although flint, formerly used in the making of flint glass, was superseded by sand. The flint glass of the Birmingham district contains a larger amount of lead than similar glass made elsewhere, giving added lustre and brilliance to the glass.).

The firm of F. & C. Osler were among the earliest glass-makers to experiment with Siemens' patent fuel-saving furnaces introduced from the Continent. For the Crystal Palace this firm made the spectacular central fountain. These Birmingham craftsmen were also responsible for the candelabra for Mahomet's tomb at Medina, the famous religious centre of the Middle East.

Notes

1. S. Timmins (ed.), *Birmingham and the Midland Hardware District* (1866).
2. W.H.B. Court (Professor of Economic History at the University of Birmingham), *The Rise of the Midland Industries 1600-1838* (Oxford University Press, 1938).
3. Told to Joan Zuckerman by the architect Holland Hobbis, who remembered seeing the cases when a young child.
4. The term 'pinchbottle' is applied to bottles with pinched, or indented, sides.

11. Railway Mania

A year before the world's first passenger-carrying railway, the Stockton and Darlington line, opened in 1825 a proposal was made for connecting Birmingham with London by rail. A company was formed and within hours 2,500 shares had been taken up — but the scheme fell through so that it was not until 1835 that an Act was finally passed for construction of the railroad. Work began at the London end two months later.

London to Birmingham

The coming of the railway was a victory not only for engineering skill but for the courage and persistence shown in the face of bitter opposition from landowners, canal shareholders and others. When local people objected to railways there were costly delays: one vicar allowed the railway over his land in return for a promise of four bridges — (he later received £20,000 from the company for *not* building them!). Land was expensive and the London-Birmingham railway sometimes paid for it at the rate of £6,000 a mile.

Opponents of the railways treated the whole matter with anger, ridicule and contempt. Contemporary writers declared that 'nothing could be more palpably absurd than the prosprect held out of locomotives travelling twice as fast as stage coaches'. Smoke from the trains, they claimed, would injure the fleeces of sheep; sparks would set fire to properties along the track; horses would bolt and cows would stop giving milk.

William Murdoch, whilst employed in Cornwall as Matthew Boulton's expert, built himself a small steam car which greatly interested an eccentric Cornishman named Richard

103

35. Railway navvies making a cutting through the hillside at Tring, in Hertfordshire, on the London to Birmingham line which opened in 1838. Vast quantities of excavated material had to be pushed in wheelbarrows up the steep sides.

Trevithick. Murdoch's design was copied and improved, and Trevithick took out a patent for it. Neither Boulton nor Watt had shown any faith in the steam car and refused to back its manufacture. It was George Stephenson's famous *Rocket* design of 1829 which became the model for all later steam locomotives.

Engineered by Stephenson

George Stephenson and his son Robert engineered the 112½ mile London to Birmingham line — the first true main railway line in the world. The cost was estimated at £2,500,000 but the final figure was nearly double that (£57 million at today's prices).

The line was opened in sections, as the track was completed — the first section opened to traffic on 27 July 1837, and covered the 24 miles between Euston Station in London to Boxmoor in Hertfordshire. With the Grand Junction Railway, a company also formed in 1833, this new line linked Liverpool and Manchester (via Birmingham) with London.

By 1846 the three railways — the Grand Junction, the Liverpool and Manchester and the London to Birmingham — united to form the London and North Western Railway — 'The

104

Premier Line', as it became known. Soon after the amalgamation the new company moved its scattered engineering works into a single unit at the village of Crewe. Soon, Crewe became a thriving railway town and until railway nationalisation the LNWR even managed the town's gas and water supplies.

By the mid-1800s all the railway companies were running at a profit. The canal shareholders' bitter opposition vanished and not only city businessmen but also the general public

36. Two early railway prints from the collection of Mr and Mrs M.G. Powell exhibited at the Victoria and Albert Museum in 1974.

GRAND ENTRANCE TO THE LONDON AND BIRMINGHAM RAILWAY.

London and Birmingham Railway   Views of the Euston Arch and a train   Anonymous   Engraving, coloured by hand

clamoured to buy railway shares. Two miles out of Birmingham, at Saltley, the Metropolitan Railway Carriage and Wagon Works was built alongside the main line in 1838. Other similar works soon opened and these Birmingham factories made railway rolling stock not only for the UK, but also for the new railways being built in Canada, Australia and Europe.

Birmingham's
first
station

When the London to Birmingham tracks were constructed by the engineers and their contractors, architects and builders were simultaneously clearing acres of ground — much of it slum housing — to bring the trains to the centre. The first station, built on the eastern fringe of the city, was an elegant building and hotel known as Curzon Street Terminus. It was designed by Philip Hardwick as an opposite number to his renowned £35,000 Doric portico at Euston (demolished in 1962 in spite of much public protest). The central stations of New Street and Snow Hill were built a few years later — New Street on a low-lying site known as The Froggery. This area had been one of the first Jewish settlements outside London after the Jews were permitted by Cromwell to return to England. Some gravestones from The Froggery site were moved to a small plot of land opposite the junction of George Road and Islington Row where they can still be seen over the top of a brick wall.

On 17 September 1838 the entire railroad from London to Birmingham's Curzon Street station was opened to passenger traffic. The boys from the public school at Rugby had the day off to watch the trains go through Rugby on the line to Birmingham, and on the opening of the line to the public the *Gazette* newspaper commented:

> Birmingham will thus be brought within six if not five hours of the capital; it remains only for those in this town, with whom is the power, to prepare such facilities of communication with the heart of the town as are requisite, and vast benefit cannot fail to result to all classes of the inhabitants.

When the Birmingham slums were cleared away so that the new station could be built on central sites, Joseph Chamberlain (see Chapter 15) was much criticised in some quarters for

106

failing to provide new accommodation for families made homeless.

Perhaps the quaintest summing-up of the new railway scene can be found in an anonymous book in a series called *Railroadiana*, published from Stationers' Court, London, in 1838. Introducing what he calls his 'picturesque, biographical, historical, legendary and antiquarian sketches' of the London-Birmingham line, the author compares the railway with earlier horse carriages and says:

> Be it remembered that there is no walking the hills, no 'pulling up' to take a lunch or a glass of ale, nor going slow to give the horses their wind. That system is likely to be annihilated . . . however much we may cling to old fashions and old customs we have no doubt that this opening of a new era to 'locomotive' minds will be hailed with satisfaction by the great body of the British people . . . it is not too much to hope that a pocket compass will be found desirable as a matter of entertainment and valuable for its utility.

107

In the same way that canals proliferated in the eighteenth century, so a network of railways covered the country by the middle of the following century. Cheap and rapid transport changed the physical aspect of Birmingham, bringing industrial prosperity and a constantly increasing population. The massive slum-clearing and excavating which preceded the laying of railway lines proved helpful to the newly designed sewage system. By 1851, eighteen miles of main sewers — lying fourteen feet underground — and over forty miles of ordinary brick sewers had been laid in Birmingham. Few other cities could match such progress in public health measures.

The introduction of branch railway lines, electric trams, buses and cycles enabled men and their families to work in the city centre but to live in the green belt of suburbs. Later private cars brought an end to these local train services on many suburban lines — now, however, after an interval of some years there are suggestions that plans might have to be drawn up to reopen some local railway lines to relieve road congestion, or even to build an underground train network serving Birmingham.[1]

What has very recently happened is the inauguration of a railway line that crosses the entire city from near Sutton Coldfield in the north-east to Longbridge in the south-west. This entailed £8 million alterations to old track and signalling — and the construction of three electrified cross-overs in the New Street station area. New stations have been built at the University and Longbridge. Five Ways station (closed since 1944) and Bournville have now been rebuilt to modern amenity standards.

New Street Station is today one of the country's outstanding modern railway termini. Every day this Birmingham station handles 600 trains and over 60,000 passengers. From New Street there are more train connections to other cities and towns than from any other station in the UK.

Note

1. John Morris Jones, Headmaster of the George Dixon Junior School, Birmingham, in his *Maps of Birmingham* (published by the City of Birmingham Education Department, 1975).

108

12. Civic Progress

On 5 November 1838, a Charter of Incorporation made Birmingham a parliamentary borough. This enabled the town to have an elected town council, with a mayor. The first town council chose as the insignia of authority the arms of the historic family of de Bermingham, dating from about the twelfth century, plus a single word motto — 'Forward', which remains to the present day.

The Charter of Incorporation

However, despite the status of Incorporation it took a further nine years for Birmingham to achieve effective powers to run its own affairs. This was because various districts each had their own administrators, known as Street Commissioners (of whom fifty had been appointed in 1769 to administer Birmingham) and they still had control of street lighting, markets, public works and repairs. The last Chairman of the Birmingham Street Commissioners was Richard T. Cadbury, a Quaker member of the chocolate-making firm. He was a greatly respected citizen of Birmingham, often referred to as 'King Richard', and he served as a Street Commissioner for half a century.

It is to Birmingham's credit that during the ineffective years when the town council was little more than a debating society and the Street Commissioners retained their powers — and the rates were miniscule — the town built public baths, a mental hospital and a prison by raising financial loans from the public.

The Street Commissioners bought the old Manorial rights which permitted them to run their own market in the city centre. For this purpose they built a great hall, with a 500-

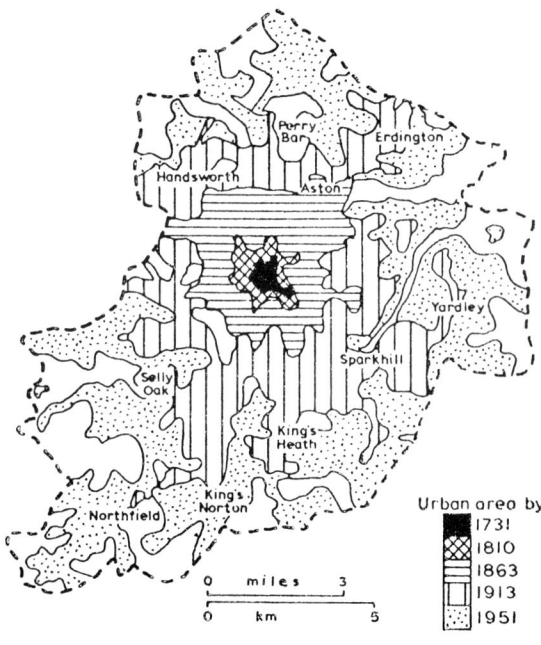

38. Stages in the expansion of Birmingham (left) and a map of the main relief features and sub-regions of the West Midlands.

foot-long roof arching over a Classical rectangular building. A great Doric porch supported the central arch of the entrance and this Market Hall continued to serve Birmingham well until the roof was destroyed during the last war. The hall was then demolished to make way for today's spectacular Bull Ring development.

A beautiful Town Hall

The Commissioners also built a distinguished Town Hall — a neoclassical interpretation of the Temple of Castor and Pollux in Rome. This design, by Hansom and Welsh, was preferred to a design submitted by Barry, the architect of the House of Commons. (Nowadays, Hansom is better known for designing the Hansom cab than for Birmingham's beautiful Town Hall.)

Whilst the Town Hall was under construction a small group of Commissioners bought up and cleared the ground around

110

the building to provide 'a respectable setting'. Part of this site, now known as Chamberlain Square, still provides an open space in the heart of the city. It proved the first of many occasions when Birmingham authorities had the foresight to buy central property for future town-planning purposes.

The buildings of the City of Birmingham have recently attracted attention in the face of threats of further demolition — already far too much of the architectural heritage of the city has been sacrificed to the builder and business speculators. Part of the vigorous new interest in preservation is due to a newly established and thriving local Victorian Society and the activities of a longer-established Georgian group.

The Victorian city centre buildings once showed remarkable variety of styles, most of them Continental in origin, including French châteaux, Flemish mansions and German castles. Ruskin's fashionable book *The Stones of Venice* inspired a variety of Italian-type villas and conservatories. Many are amusing, some imposing.

Simultaneously, the old Georgian tradition continued in many streets, public houses and in occasional large buildings such as the County Court building which surprisingly, is more or less contemporary with its High Victorian neighbour, the Victoria Law Courts.

The Georgian-style public house, with its ornate 'iron convenience' (lavatory), is very characteristic of older Birmingham. Many of the early taverns were impressive in size and setting — for instance Showell's *Dictionary of Birmingham* (1885) says of the Aston Cross Tavern:

> it was opened as a licenced house and tea gardens in 1775 ... of late years it has been a favourite resort of all classes of athletes but by being closely built around it has lost much of the attraction which drew our grandfathers to its shady arbours when on country pleasure bent.

Looking at industrial Aston Cross today (HP Sauce factory, Ansells Brewery, broadcasting studios etc.) makes Showell's description almost impossible to visualise.

111

In wrought-iron and cast-iron work, including decorative gates and clock towers, Birmingham achieved such distinction that a new nickname was coined for her simply on account of the lavatories — the 'Home of the Iron Convenience'. At the end of the nineteenth century, and in reaction against Victorian baroque, a new style of artistic craftsmanship, based on simplicity combined with functional value, was favoured by many industrialists and good 'art nouveau' buildings appeared in the city.

First garden city

Meantime, new architectural and planning ideas were gaining support throughout the country, particularly those encouraging landscaping with trees, parks and gardens to give industrial workers a pleasant environment. Wealthy people were well served by the Calthorpe estate in Edgbaston, the first of England's garden cities, and this estate continued to expand and exert considerable influence not only on new Birmingham developments (such as the Bournville and Harborne estates) but also on suburban developments throughout Great Britain. Today's new towns incorporate many ideas and concepts of planning and landscaping developed in eighteenth- and nineteenth-century Birmingham.

The elegance and grandeur of Birmingham's public buildings was in sharp contrast to the working-class homes of the nineteenth century. Speculative builders erected over 2,000 'courts' of small houses near the city centre and by 1830 a cholera epidemic was so grave that it led to a government inquiry — the first of its kind — into housing conditions for factory workers. Each of these Victorian court houses cost only about £60 to build and was rented at between 2s. 6d. (12½p) and 4s. (20p) a week. They had neither drainage nor lighting, inside or out, and the streets and yards were left unpaved. Through ventilation was abandoned in favour of a double row of houses sharing a mutual back wall, seldom more than 4½ inches thick and these Siamese twins of houses have since become known as back-to-backs.

Courts and alleys

A back-to-back has a front house with a door which opens into the street, whilst the door of the back house opens into a courtyard. The lavatory, water pump and wash-house for both were in this courtyard. Occasionally as many as twenty houses shared one courtyard, but usually a street was so

112

arranged that four houses formed a pair of back-to-backs, and shared a courtyard with an opposite group of four houses.

As Frederick Alderson says in his book *View North*, back-to-backs became 'crowded in confined courts and alleys, sometimes even built side by side; some could be approached only through tunnels a yard wide, eight feet high and up to thirty feet long'. Living conditions were very bad, epidemics raged and many children died.

Because slum dwellings were exacting such heavy health penalties from the working classes George Cadbury[1] decided in 1879 to move his chocolate factory four miles outside the built-up areas to Bournville. There he established a model industrial village where stretches of parkland, with woods and lakes, covered as large an area as did the individual houses. The Cadburys' highly practical enterprise was not confined to houses and amenities for employees only, as was the case in some subsequent housing estate developments. From the start Bournville was created for a mixed and balanced society and it continues today to be admired and studied by visitors from all over the industrialised world.

113

Despite the hardships suffered by the Birmingham workers – including punishing hours and bad factory conditions for men, women *and* children of eleven onwards – the city forged ahead in dramatic fashion from the mid-nineteenth century. Birmingham's civic progress became second to none in the kingdom. In 1890 an American observer remarked that Birmingham was the 'best-governed city in the world'. Much of the credit for civic improvements goes to Mr J. Pigott Smith, who was appointed City Surveyor in 1852. This outstanding civil engineer had previously worked for the Birmingham Street Commissioners for thirteen years. Mr Pigott Smith was famed as much for his new system of sanitation as for his road-building and improvements schemes. Deputations from other large cities at home and abroad 'visited Birmingham in order to learn the methods of paving, cleaning and draining which were practised there'.

As Carlyle
saw the city

Thomas Carlyle, the Scottish historian and man of letters, lived for a short time in Birmingham. A letter written to his brother in 1824 gives an interesting picture of the contemporary industrial city:

Birmingham I have now tried for a reasonable time, and I cannot complain of being tired of it. As a town it is pitiful enough – a mean congeries of bricks, including one or two large capitalists, some hundred of minor ones and, perhaps, a hundred and twenty thousand sooty artisans in metals and chemical produce. The streets are ill-built, ill-paved, always flimsy in their aspect – often poor, sometimes miserable. Not above one or two of them are paved with flagstones at the sides; and to walk upon the little egg-shaped, slippery flints that supply their places is something like a penance. Yet withal it is interesting from some of the commons or lanes that spot and intersect the green, woody, undulating environs to view this city of Tubal Cain. Torrents of thick smoke, with ever and anon a burst of dingy flame, are issuing from a thousand funnels. 'A thousand hammers fall by turns'. You hear the clank of innumerable steam engines, the rumbling of cars and vans, and the hum of men interrupted by the sharper rattle of some canal boat loading or disloading, or, perhaps, some fierce explosion when the cannon founders are proving their new-made ware. I have seen their rolling mills, their pol-

114

ishing of teapots, and buttons and gun-barrels, and fire-
shovels and swords, and all manner of toys and tackle . . .
the whole is not without its attractions, as well as repul-
sions, of which when we meet, I will preach to you at
large.

Note

1. It was George Cadbury and his brother Richard, sons of the
original founder of the firm John Cadbury, who in 1866 imported
from Holland a machine which produced a good cocoa essence, enabling the trade to prosper from that point on. John Cadbury had
started by selling fifteen kinds of chocolate and ten of cocoa, largely
as a form of medicine.

13. Industrial Expansion

Increase in
machine power

In the early nineteenth century steam engines capable of blowing furnaces, pumping water and driving machinery of all kinds were quickly becoming commonplace in Birmingham's metal industries. By 1817 this new mechanical power had allowed the weight of tilt hammers to increase from a few hundredweights to two or three tons each. Fuel could now be mechanically lifted to the top of blast furnaces and no longer had to be hauled up inclined platforms.

Most of Birmingham and the Black Country's exported metal goods were destined for America. The American market was critical for English Midland towns both before, during and after the Wars of Independence. The American settlers were mainly engaged in agriculture or in making cotton textiles; labour costs were very high, steam power still unknown and communications primitive. It was therefore some time before America was able to meet all her own basic requirements.

Consequently, such things as agricultural implements, lamps and firearms, and the household equipment known as hollow-ware — items like kettles, saucepans and frying pans — were exported from England in large quantity. Hand-made nails were sent out in such volume that about a quarter of a million nails, produced in and around Birmingham and sold mostly through Birmingham-based ironmongers, went to America in one year alone — 1812.

When steam power was eventually introduced in America towards the middle of the nineteenth century it sparked off an inventive boom in designing new machinery to make mass-produced goods. Some of these new machines had a

116

quick feedback to the Midlands and patents were bought and adapted to meet the needs of Birmingham's industrial expansion. The Boulton and Watt foundry was now working to full capacity, as well as serving as a training centre for engineers throughout the land. This was the first and, for a long time, the only such foundry entirely geared to make engines — just as the Soho Works was the first factory specifically designed to make metal goods.

Boulton and Watt engines were being exported to many places overseas; for instance, between 1802 and 1852 the firm built 148 cane-mill engines for crushing sugar cane. Of these, 56 went to Jamaica, 54 to British Guiana, 12 to Trinidad, 5 to Grenada, three to Brazil and one each to St Croix, Tobago, St Lucia, Surinam, Georgia and New Orleans.

Exporting from Soho

Unlike other industrial towns specialising in textiles, or some other single industry, Birmingham continued to prosper when trade was declining elsewhere in the country. Not until after the victory at Waterloo in 1815 did Birmingham feel the force of a national economic slump, largely due to a sharp drop in government contracts.

By 1817, following the wars in France, nearly half of Birmingham's 60,000 citizens were out of work and dependent on charity. The following year this petition was sent to Parliament, signed by 11,000 desperate men: 'We implore your Honourable House to remove the cause of misery, whatever it may be, and we cannot think that your Honourable House cannot remove it.'

Protests by the unemployed

Newhall Hill was the chief rallying point for Birmingham political demonstrations of protest, but no help was forthcoming that year or the next and the grim situation grew worse. In the decade which followed recovery from the slump came slowly, for trade was still slack and prices high. In 1830 Thomas Attwood, a local banker, suggested a change in national economic policy based upon the issue of inconvertible paper money. Attwood believed in the principle of a managed currency which did not depend on gold, and in encouraging productive expenditure in the hope of averting a further threatened slump. Moreover, Attwood urged that a

117

large proportion of members of the House of Commons should be men with practical business and banking experience — it was his belief that this would result in better financial control of the nation's economy.

Attwood gathered a group of fellow townsmen into the Political Union for the Protection of Public Rights. In its first year 9,000 Birmingham men joined this union and considerable support came from other manufacturing towns. The union's main objective was to correct a system which gave many insignificant towns and villages in England the right to be represented by an elected member of Parliament, whereas many important developing industrial centres, Birmingham among them, had no member and consequently no political representation at all.

Birmingham's first MPs

The Birmingham union was the first organised movement to campaign for a change in the constitution and function of the old-fashioned Houses of Parliament and it gave rise to the introduction of the Reform Bill. On 4 June 1831 this first Reform Bill sought to create 22 new boroughs, each with the right to send one elected member to Parliament.

Birmingham people were much concerned with the Bill's progress and were so enraged when the Bill, having successfully passed through the Commons, was thrown out by the House of Lords that there were fears of an armed revolution. The Duke of Wellington, then Prime Minister, resigned and the Whigs (later replaced by the term Liberal) returned to power with a guarantee in their pocket that this vitally important Bill would be passed in the Lords with, if the need arose, new peers created to help get the measure accepted. On its second time around, however, the Reform Bill was passed without trouble by both Houses of Parliament (1832).

There were great celebrations in Birmingham. A jubilant crowd, about 200,000 strong, formed a procession four miles long, cheered on by brass bands, to an open-air rally on Newhall Hill. One member of the House of Lords declared that the Birmingham union 'saved the country from disaster by advocating union, justice, reason and law and bending over backwards to stop the people carrying out a threat to arm in self-defence'. An election followed and the banker

118

Attwood and Joshua Scholefield, both radicals (a term historically applied to political reformers) and both influential leaders of the Political Union, were elected without opposition to serve as Birmingham's first Members of Parliament.

Alas, in practice the first Reform Bill proved sadly inadequate. In 1838 a 'People's Charter' was drawn up by members of a movement which sought an extension of political power for the working classes. Chartism, as it became known, campaigned for a vote for all adult males, a secret ballot, annual elections, the abolition of property-owning qualifications for MPs, payment of MPs and the setting up of equal electoral districts. In 1848 the Chartists planned a mass march to present a new petition,[1] but due to the stringent measures taken to restrain them, and disunity within the Party, the march proved a damp squib. By 1858 the movement had petered out. However, the Chartist agitations had important repercussions since they encouraged and strengthened the emerging trade unions.

The Chartist agitations

Bishop Westcott gives a moving account of these dramatic and important years when Birmingham played a leading role in agitating for political reform. He writes:

> Those were stirring years. We who passed through them felt that the old order was changing, and that a revolution was going on about us, the issue of which could not be forseen. The first event of which I have a clear recollection was the meeting of the Political Union on Newhall Hill in 1831. I can see still the Crown and Royal Standard in front of the platform, which reassured my childish heart, startled by wild words of violence and rebellion. The Chartist movement followed soon after. I listened to Fergus O'Connor, and I saw the blackened ruins in the Bull Ring guarded by soldiers. Then came the Corn Law agitation and the Factory Acts. They were stirring times; political, economic and, looking forward already to the work of a priest and teacher, I watched them with the keenest interest.

The Chartist meeting in the Bull Ring, July 1839, to which Westcott refers, ended in violence, with buildings set on fire and several deaths. The angry crowd was enraged by the pre-

Clashes with London police

119

sence of a body of armed London police, sent by government order, which showed considerable brutality in handling the crowds. Alderman Joseph Sturge, one of Birmingham's Quaker figureheads (see also Chapter 16) led a strong protest at a council meeting against the police action. He saw the danger in the police becoming a national body with so much authority and power that their presence would only add fuel to the flames instead of smothering them.

Sturge asserted that 'for some days he could hardly express his feelings with anything like temper' and, at the Council meeting, he proposed a formal declaration 'emphatically protesting against the attempt to engraft one of the most pernicious institutions of continental tyranny on the English system of representation'.

Meanwhile, Thomas Attwood — the local banker MP already referred to — complained to Parliament that the Police Act (rushed through because of the Chartist agitation) gave control of local forces to the Home Office, although local councils were made to raise the rates to pay for the force. Attwood complained that the London police sent to Birmingham had been armed with sabres and cutlasses which he feared 'would be the commencement of a system of "gendarmerie", centred in London and spreading through every parish in England'.

The Chartist movement was very much a working-class movement. It is therefore strange to find Joseph Sturge — a prosperous corn merchant — accepted as a leader. But Sturge was not only a devout Quaker; he worked hard to achieve the liberation and education of the West Indian negro. This, and the stand he made against the London police, won the admiration of the Chartists.

Changes in manufacturing

This was a time of great change in industry, sometimes as a result of new discoveries, at other times through changing fashions and markets. For instance, in 1840 the jewellers discovered how to use an electro-plating process for gilding and silver-plating, and the result of this was a substantial increase in cheap, mass-produced jewellery.[2] The Elkington brothers, a classic name in the trade, developed an electro-plating factory, a little to the north of St Philip's Church,

120

from where they turned out thousands of electro-plated spoons, forks and fish cutlery.

Further vigour came to the jewellery trade when new sources of gold supplies came in from the mines of Australia and Colorado and silver from the mines of Nevada, in the western mountain area of America.

In the button trade fashions were changing and metal buttons were becoming replaced by fabric buttons (with shanks made from ivory or canvas) and porcelain buttons, whilst still others were made of glass, wood, horn, bone, jet, leather and pearl. All these different types were made in such great quantity that Birmingham became the centre of the button trade for the entire country.

New methods of heating and lighting with the use of gas vastly increased the manufacture of brass and copper pipes. At one Birmingham factory alone, that of R.W. Winfield in Cambridge Street, many hundreds of workers were kept busy making miles of gas piping (this factory and the glass firm of Chance Bros. were among the first to provide part-time education for their young employees in schools run on the factory premises). Hollow metal tubes were also in demand for fashionable objects such as brass bedsteads, cornice poles, firescreens and other Victoriana.

One entirely new industry — machine tools — was getting into its stride by the middle of the nineteenth century, both in Birmingham and Manchester. The production of standard gauges, measuring machines, classified screws and screw threads proved of the utmost value to Birmingham industry.

Importance of machine tools

Apart from the constant progress that was being made in all branches of engineering, discoveries in chemistry and physics were quickly taken up. Soon after the middle of the century cobalt, citric acid, explosives, phosphates and photographic products were all being made in Birmingham.

As industry expanded, so did the population. By 1870 there were a quarter of a million people living in Birmingham, most of them employed in engineering workshops and factories. Many children were at work, some as young as six or seven.

These children were employed in the small workshops and were expected to put in the same twelve-hour day for six full days a week as the adult craftsmen. A skilled man in his workshop earned about £1.50 a week, the women less than this, and the children got no more than two shillings (10p) for their 84-hour week.[3]

As the nineteenth century drew to its close there were few families in the land who did not make daily use of many products that were 'made in Birmingham'.

Notes

1. Nine years earlier Attwood had presented a petition formulated at a big Chartist meeting in Birmingham, but it was rejected.

2. In 1978 what was widely known as 'the corner shop' in Birmingham's jewellery quarter (it stood at the junction of Great Hampton Street and Kenyon Street) closed after nearly two hundred years' service to the trade, in the last century and a half mainly supplying electro-platers. The shop was started in 1785 by William Gunn, to supply salts to the jewellery trade. Gunn later joined the Canning family and it is this concern which is today a leading trade supplier.

3. Dr Marie B. Rowlands, *A History of Industry in Birmingham* (City of Birmingham Education Department, 1977).

14. Preachers of Influence

A tradition of political agitation from the pulpit was an enduring legacy from the great Dr Joseph Priestley (see also Chapter 8). By the 1870s a spiritual revival movement was led by George Dawson, a Nonconformist minister. Thundering from his Sunday pulpit, Dawson proclaimed that 'our people live in filth and disease, large parts of our great city are a shame and disgrace.'

Dawson first came to Birmingham in 1844 to preach in the Mount Zion Chapel, in Graham Street. The following year his friends built him a new chapel called the Church of the Saviour, 'where no pledge was required, of minister or congregation; no form of belief was implied by membership; and no difference in creed was allowed to bar union in practical Christian work'.

In his sermons Dawson continually called upon his congregation to join him in the struggle 'to improve conditions in the town and the quality of life enjoyed by its citizens'. It was said of Dawson that:

> He would talk to his congregation about Avery's scales and about yard measures, about tea and sugar, about adulterated mustard, and about butter half of which was fat, about stock-taking and long credit, about dressing shop windows; about all the details of doings of a scoundrel who had been tried a day or two before for his transactions in connection with a fraudulent stock company, about dress and jewellery, about dinners and evening parties, about all the follies and sins and vanities of the day ... He was not a preaching man, but a man preaching. Or,

to put the truth in another way, he preached not as a dying man to dying men — that was the old idea of preaching — but as a living man to living men who found life no simple or easy matter.

After the consecration of St Chad's Roman Catholic Cathedral in 1838, Birmingham became the centre of Roman Catholicism in England — a position she held for many years, partly due to the proximity of the great collegiate institution at Oscott. In 1848 the town became a See of Rome and the Rev. Dr Ullathorne was appointed Roman Catholic Bishop of Birmingham.

The Oratory of St Phillip Neri was founded very shortly afterwards by Dr John Henry Newman, who had arrived in Birmingham three years after Dawson. It found a temporary home in Alcester Street until, in 1852, an Oratory was built in Hagley Road. Construction of this famous and beautiful Birmingham building took place between 1903 and 1909.

Dr Newman, as Birmingham's first Cardinal (the highest office in the Catholic Church next to the Pope) was a very different religious leader from George Dawson. Although brought up a Calvinist, Newman joined the Church of England and became one of the figureheads of the Oxford Movement which sought to strengthen and revitalise the Established Church. Together with Edward Pusey and John Keble, two other clerics and leaders of the Oxford Movement, Newman tried to purify the Anglican doctrine, to bring back some of the pre-Reformation ritual, with its accompanying splendour and romance. It was this movement which gave birth to that branch within the Established Church of England now known as Anglo-Catholic.

Newman's spiritual upheavals were turbulent. He eventually left the Church of England to become a Roman Catholic. When, as Cardinal Newman, he moved to Birmingham, the Oratory became a centre of spiritual influence which attracted many visitors. It was here that Newman spent many years searching for answers to spiritual problems and here, too, that he wrote his great poem, *The Dream of Gerontius*. This

40. One of Birmingham's many Nonconformist chapels, in a typical industrial street setting of small workshops and a paper merchant's warehouse with arched entrance.

poem was later to be used by Elgar as the text for a work composed expressly for the Birmingham Musical Festival in 1900.

The Nonconformist Dr R.W. Dale, minister of the parent chapel of the Congregationalists in Carr's Lane for nearly forty years, carried on in the style of Priestley and Dawson. He plunged into political activity at both civic and national levels and, like Dawson, made himself familiar with the day-to-day commercial matters which preoccupied the members of his congregation.

Dr Dale's politics

Dr Dale fought hard for a better standard of living, physical as well as spiritual, believing that slum clearance was just as important as delivering good sermons to packed congregations. As far afield as Australia and America, in both of which he preached and lectured, he was famous simply as

125

'Dr Dale of Birmingham'. His home congregation feared, loved and admired him and he had great respect for his congregation. He pronounced the skilled artisan of Birmingham 'the best hearer he had ever found — ready to take and appreciate the strongest thinking that could be offered him'.

Dale was opposed to the amalgamation of religious denominations. He did not support the Birmingham Free Church Council, which was attempting to organise co-operation amongst all the Nonconformist churches. He had some sympathy for its aim but none at all for the procedure it adopted, which, he felt, would debase the religious integrity of the Church and water it down to a mere political body.

By the end of the nineteenth century, Birmingham supported six Anglican churches, including St Philip's; a Quaker church; Unitarian, Baptist and Methodist chapels; a Roman Catholic oratory and the new Roman Catholic Church of St Peter's — built to resemble a warehouse from outside and tucked into the corner of Brass House Lane because, when it was built, anti-Roman Catholic feeling still ran high. A new Jewish Synagogue was erected at the time; some believe that it was endowed by Lord George Gordon — who was known as the 'Birmingham Moses'.

The Gordon riots

The eccentric Lord George Gordon became a Member of Parliament in his youth. He first supported the government, then joined the Opposition. Finally he quarrelled with both parties, giving rise to the saying that three parties existed — the Ministry, the Opposition and Lord George Gordon. He is remembered for leading the anti-Roman Catholic riots in London, known as the 'Gordon riots'. Lord George adopted the Jewish faith and lived in hiding as one of the Jewish community in Birmingham for nearly four months. He was then arrested, found guilty of libelling the Queen of France and sent to Newgate Prison.

126

15. Joseph Chamberlain

Birmingham's reputation as an important centre of radical thinking held firm throughout the nineteenth century. It was strengthened by two eminent middle-class industrialists of strong Nonconformist convictions and radical political opinions. These men were John Bright and Joseph Chamberlain – names which live on in the Birmingham of today, not only in the naming of thoroughfares and buildings but in the spirit of the city.

Names to commemorate

John Bright, a Quaker, was a partner in a Manchester cotton-spinning firm. In 1847 he became Manchester's Liberal Member of Parliament. He took the lead in a movement calling for parliamentary reform, and a campaign for the repeal of the Corn Laws. Whilst a Manchester MP, Bright opposed the Crimean War and spoke out against Palmerston's action in China and Persia. In consequence, he lost his parliamentary seat in April 1857. Birmingham, in need of a new MP, elected him without contest in August of the same year.

Joseph Chamberlain (1836-1914) was elected a Liberal Member of Parliament for Birmingham in 1876. Bright and Chamberlain joined forces to press for wider electoral franchise – these Birmingham men have been called 'the first professional politicians'. Bright and Chamberlain – who was commonly called 'Radical Joe' – became figures of national importance, successfully holding office as Ministers of the Crown.

Professional politicians

Chamberlain originally came from London to look after his family's interests in the manufacture of mass-produced screws. The Nonconformist minister George Dawson (see

127

previous chapter) persuaded Chamberlain to stand for election to the town council. He won the seat with the help of J.T. Bunce, one of the great editors of the famous provincial newspaper, the *Birmingham Post*. This newspaper remained one of Chamberlain's most loyal and influential life-long supporters. Intelligent, well informed articles pressing for municipal reform and backing the local radical leaders were frequently published in the newspaper. When the Liberal Party splintered and one part of it formed a movement to oppose Gladstone's Irish Home Rule policy, the leading articles in the *Birmingham Post* contributed to its success. Eventually this new movement became affiliated with the Conservatives under the name of the Birmingham Conservative and Unionist Political Association.

It was Chamberlain's ambition to see Birmingham become an outstanding example of an efficiently run provincial town. To this end his experience as a businessman in the screw-manufacturing firm of Guest, Keen and Nettlefold proved useful. So, too, did his unshakeable confidence in the importance and dignity of municipal life which he expressed in the view that Birmingham society was 'superior in earnestness, sincerity and natural intelligence to any other'.

Organised by Chamberlain, the Assize Court was brought to Birmingham, which necessitated the building of the Victoria Law Courts, a most imposing building in red brick and terra-cotta, designed by Aston Webb and Ingress Bell. New town improvement Acts were passed by central government and at the time England enjoyed a period of relative peace — as well as considerable prosperity. In Birmingham six joint-stock banks and a branch of the Bank of England were established. By 1889 Birmingham had achieved full city status.

It was Chamberlain who persuaded the somewhat reluctant city council to buy the local gasworks. It proved a very sound investment and the council spent the profit from the gas-works on buying property in the centre of the town. This made it possible, during the three years of Chamberlain's office as mayor (1873-6) to plan the development of Cor-poration Street and New Street. The area was leased, not sold, and soon became a highly respectable business centre and one fashionable for shopping.

At no cost to the ratepayers, six parks were presented to the town by Birmingham citizens. The most important of these is Cannon Hill Park, presented by Mrs Ryland (she also played an important part in the purchase of Aston Hall and its gardens for the city).

Again thanks to Chamberlain, the city council bought the Elan Valley in Wales to supplement Birmingham's inadequate water supply. Reservoirs were built there and an aqueduct, 73 miles long, provided the town with soft Welsh water to the great advantage of many industrial processes, particularly those of the metal industries.

Loyalty to
Radical Joe
The drive, enterprise and foresight of Chamberlain made Birmingham the best-governed city in the country. In return, Birmingham provided Radical Joe with solid support throughout his very unusual political career. His public speeches on what Enoch Powell[1] refers to as 'his classic stage' — Birmingham Town Hall — were political occasions of the utmost national importance.

'Brummagems' needed conditions favourable to trade. This was their political motivation. In consequence they stood against the King in the days of the Civil War, and later against the upheaval of revolution as seen in France. The citizens of Birmingham were content to continue trading with America throughout the struggle for independence. They disliked the progressive spirit, as epitomised by members of the Lunar Society (see Chapter 8), particularly Dr Priestley, and were not in favour of any measure which limited free trade. This need for stability drew many Birmingham people towards John Wesley's Methodist teachings, which emphasised the need for each person to accept their allotted social status in life.

The years 1885-6, when Gladstone suffered the defeat of his first Home Rule for Ireland Bill,[2] formed a fulcrum point in Joseph Chamberlain's career. Not only was Chamberlain himself opposed to the concept of home rule for Ireland but the people of Birmingham were solidly behind him in this fight. Instead, Joe Chamberlain favoured the idea of federalism (i.e. associations of states which, though autonomous in home affairs, combine on wider national and international

130

policy). Today, many may think that this would have been a proper solution and one which would have avoided many current problems.

The legacy of Dr Priestley's dictum of 'the greatest happiness for the greatest number' — a slogan taken up by Chamberlain in a speech in 1894 — was basic to Birmingham people's philosophy. Chamberlain's federalist policy was one which he considered capable of being extended to the whole of the British Empire, with an Imperial Parliament at Westminster (who knows what might have stemmed from such a world-wide federation in the twentieth century?).

The townspeople of Birmingham were confident that Chamberlain's stand was based on a determination to improve the lot of the working classes — and this improvement was to come about by preserving the prosperity of Great Britain so that her voice should be powerful throughout the Empire.

Chamberlain's passionate desire to strengthen ties between Britain and the colonies (he wished to safeguard, and even expand, the British Empire) caused him to act in such a way that troubles in South Africa increased and gave rise to the Boer War. The 'Brummies' still backed their hero Radical Joe, even though he had by then become a member of the Conservative Party.

Campaign for tariff reform

Because he opposed Chamberlain, Lloyd George — the great Liberal leader and statesman (1863-1945) — got so rough a hearing when he spoke in Birmingham Town Hall about the Boer War that he had to be disguised as a policeman (his small height notwithstanding) and smuggled out through a side door!

Joe's last great campaign was for tariff reform. He aimed to keep out foreign goods by imposing taxes on them. At the same time the British Empire was to make trade agreements to the exclusive mutual benefit of countries within the Empire — particular preferential treatment was to be reserved for the mother country, Great Britain. Chamberlain believed such a policy would prevent the spectre of unemployment and a rising cost of living, which he con-

43. In 1900 the City Council visited the Elan Valley in Wales, from which water is piped 73 miles to Birmingham.

sidered was a constant threat both then and in the future. Thus a strong British Empire linked to Great Britain in some form of federation was Joseph's dream — but it was a dream he was unable to make come true.

Chamberlain's other dream, to achieve the right of all old people to receive state pensions, also failed — as did his attempt to secure compulsory and undenominational state education for all children. Both were causes dear to Joe's heart and had helped to make him the hero of the Birmingham working man. If these working men were faithful to their hero, on his part Chamberlain relied totally on this unswerving support. Without it he could never have stayed in the forefront of British politics, splitting first the Liberal and then the Conservative parties; starting the Unionist Party; becoming Britain's Colonial Secretary; and only just missing — in spite of his strange career — the position of Prime Minister. (Chamberlain's sons Austen and Neville both became statesmen and Neville Chamberlain, a Conservative MP for the Ladywood division of Birmingham, became successively Postmaster-General, Minister of Health, Chancellor of the Exchequer and Prime Minister.)

Thus the name of Joseph Chamberlain remains closely associated with Birmingham, not only because of the great advances made in town administration — amounting to a civic renaissance during his two periods as mayor — but because this city was his platform and he was their man. Without an understanding of what Chamberlain meant to Birmingham it is difficult to see why Birmingham — a place of such a vast number of different trades and highly independent working men basically radical and Nonconformist — did not give greater and quicker support to the rising Labour Party.

Trade unionism had relatively little support in the town in Joseph Chamberlain's day. The traditions of Dr Priestley, John Wesley, George Dawson and Dr Dale (see previous chapter) and, above all, Radical Joe himself kept the people in the middle of the road politically, only swinging a little left or right with the national political tide. It was not until 1924 that a Labour candidate was elected to Parliament. The trade union movement was never very strongly supported by Birmingham people.

Until as recently as the 1960s, election posters in Birmingham called for votes 'for the Conservative and Unionist Party' or just plain Unionist – not, as other areas of England, for either Conservative, Liberal or Labour. However, this style has now changed – except in the party name nationally, which is 'Conservative and Unionist'.

The eminent Joe Chamberlain died in 1914, when the First World War began. He was buried at Key Hill cemetery at the far end of Icknield Street in Birmingham.

Today the spirit of the rather sanctimonious Victorian city fathers and their families lingers evocatively about this large and lugubrious cemetery – originally a quarry supplying highly prized sand used for making cores for cast-iron moulds. When the quarry was exhausted, the city council decided to turn it into a profit-making enterprise. Thus the cemetery was built, and the cliff-face burrowed into for family mausoleums. Huge inscribed doors close the family tombs from inquisitive eyes, whilst elaborate Victorian monuments to the dead festoon the graveyard.

Notes

1. Enoch Powell, *Joseph Chamberlain* (London, Thames and Hudson, 1977).
2. Gladstone's second Home Rule Bill was passed by the Commons but thrown out by the Lords in 1893. It was not until 1914 that an act was placed on the Statute Book. This Act was superseded by the Government of Ireland Act of 1920 setting up the Irish Free State, but with the bulk of Ulster remaining united with Great Britain.

16. The Advance of Learning

Until about the middle of the nineteenth century elementary education was fragmentary to the point that scarcely half the children in Birmingham got any kind of regular schooling. Those over the age of ten or eleven were normally at work helping to support their families. The smattering of reading, writing and simple arithmetic these working children had was acquired from attendance at Sunday school. The Sunday school movement was, of course, active throughout the country and it came to Birmingham as a result of the efforts of James Luckcock, a political reformer, the Rev. C. Curtis, Rector of St Martin's Parish Church, and the Rev. J. Riland of St Mary's. The movement at once had the support of all churches, particularly the Methodists.

In the previous century Birmingham boasted some early schools giving a more or less classical type of education. These included a Free Grammar School opened in 1707; the Blue Coat Charity School of 1724, built in St Philip's Churchyard and offering orphans and poor children a good elementary education and religious instruction according to the principles of the Church of England; the Protestant Dissenting School; and, later, an energetic scholastic institution at Five Ways — not far from the city centre — called the Birmingham and Edgbaston Proprietary School to provide for proprietors' sons a school in which the advantages of a classical and commercial education could be combined.

Parents and others in the city formed the Birmingham School Association in 1850 which led directly to the setting up of a National Public School Association (the meaning of the words *public schools* have, of course, since changed). There

136

followed a Birmingham conference in 1861 devoted to 'the education of neglected and destitute children' and, shortly after, the organisation of the National Education League.

The Church of England National Society initiated regular primary schooling and thus acquired a strong grip on education for young children. A group of influential Nonconformists formed the Education League's executive committee to try to halt this trend. In 1869, the first meeting of the League was held in Birmingham. The chairman, George Dixon, was supported by a committee on which sat Joseph Chamberlain, Dr Dawson and Dr Dale (see also Chapter 14), J.T. Bunce of the *Birmingham Post*, and many other distinguished figures.

The League stopped the government framing legislation which would effectively have put all schoolchildren, irrespective of the family's religious convictions, under Church of England instruction and domination.[1] For eight years the League was extremely active throughout the country. Its objectives were:

(1) that local authorities should be compelled by law to see that sufficient school accommodation is provided for every child in their district;
(2) the cost of founding and maintaining such schools as may be required to be provided out of local rates supplemented by government grants;
(3) all schools aided by local rates to be under the management of local authorities and subject to government inspection;
(4) all schools aided by local rates' to be unsectarian;
(5) to all schools aided by local rates admission to be free;
(6) school accommodation being provided, the state or local authorities to have power to compel the attendance of children of suitable age not otherwise receiving education.

The Liberals under Gladstone's leadership passed the 1870 Education Act. This provided the first Board schools, which were to be administered by an elected board of local governors with the power to remit fees and increase accommodation in existing schools. The Nonconformists were furious

The first Board schools

44. The Chamberlain Clock Tower at the University of Birmingham. Science and engineering have given this university a very individual identity.

because, in practice, this meant that existing Church of England schools were expanded and became partially rate-supported and consequently new non-sectarian schools were not built.

To make matters worse, the governing boards were said to be 'deliberately packed with clerical members' — although many of them were only *ex officio* members. This situation, which threatened totally to obliterate Nonconformity, gave rise to a Nonconformist revolt against the government. The revolt originated at a lecture given in Birmingham and Manchester in 1871 by Dr R.W. Dale, the Birmingham pastor.

There followed mass meetings of Nonconformists throughout the country, once again demanding new schools free from denominational overtones. An awkward situation arose since in most cases this meant supporting a campaign against the Liberal Party, to which most Nonconformists belonged. The

fight for the survival of the right to dissent from the Established Church, and to keep religion separate and independent from government interference, were burning issues fraught with bitterness and hostility. The rift between Church of England members and Nonconformists grew wider and wider until it proved quite impossible to draft a new Education Act. It had to wait until many years later when some of the heat had died down.[2]

Birmingham Dissenters did not wait for the final outcome of the conflict but secured the changes they wanted in their own town. These included some interesting educational experiments. Thus, when George Dixon became Chairman of the School Board in 1876, he founded an experimental school called the Bridge Street Technical School. One comment on its influence stated:

The school was a great success. Clever boys were readily

found, and they received an excellent training in science, which at that time was hardly to be found in any secondary school. The experiment was repeated elsewhere, and School Boards in most large towns provided secondary schools of this new and valuable type. Mr. Dixon's school was largely responsible for this, for it clearly indicated that talent existed, and plenty of it, if it could only be allowed to find its way to the right place.

By 1880 there were 28 Board schools in Birmingham — handsome buildings which were admired and envied by many visitors. Each school catered for about 1,000 children. New schools, a progressive programme of teacher training, the provision of free school meals and a health service for the poor as early as 1894 won Birmingham high educational regard throughout the country. So, too, did the pioneer experiments in special educational treatment for backward children and juvenile offenders. The government next raised the school-leaving age to 12, by which time education had become the nation's most expensive social service.

Joseph Sturge's work

The success of children's Sunday schools led to the opening of the first *adult* Sunday School in 1845. It was initiated by

Joseph Sturge, the Birmingham industrialist and philanthropist. Sturge is famed for his work on behalf of the slaves of the West Indies. In Jamaica, the negroes were said to have worn the same broad-brimmed hats as he wore, which they called Sturge hats, as a token of gratitude. When he died, representatives of a number of coloured congregations sent his family a letter in which the following moving passage occurs: 'all feel that they are bereaved of a friend and benefactor whose anxiety and efforts for their welfare have never been surpassed and will ever associate the name of Sturge, in their recollection with Clarkson, Wilberforce and Buxton.'

Sturge's Sunday school in Birmingham offered instruction 'in reading the Scriptures, and in writing, to youths and young men from fourteen years of age and upwards'. Three years later Sturge opened a *women's* 'First-day School'. Notwithstanding the opposition they met from traditionalists, both the adult and women's Sunday schools flourished. Nearly half a century later a former teacher wrote:

I can remember the feeling of fear and almost awe with which we entered on our duties. The one abiding impression of my class is the affection and devotion dealt out to

46. Children using demolished slum housing to create exciting playgrounds. Photographs taken by Joan Zuckerman to encourage offers of holiday hospitality for disadvantaged city children.

me, which I had done nothing to merit, for I was very ill able to enter into the various troubles and distress. I can remember that the older members of my class lived at home under circumstances of extreme travail. Drinking fathers, faithless lovers, cruel masters made up, in their small horizon, dominant humanity . . . What we owe to Joseph Sturge, the prophet of our town and of the Society of Friends, will never be told. He sowed and watered the seed which is now a great tree, so that the birds come and lodge in its branches.

The success of the modern adult further education movement owes a great debt to Joseph Sturge's foundations — and to William White, who taught in the schools for 52 years.

A distinguished Institute

Adult education was strongly supported by the Birmingham city authorities. The Birmingham and Midland Institute, which absorbed the earlier Polytechnic Institute of 1843, was opened in 1856. Built in the Italian style, it had two sections — General and Industrial. The first section of the Institute embraced a first-class literary society, a news room, lecture programme, history and literature classes — all for the price of 21 shillings a year.

The Birmingham and Midland Institute provided unrivalled opportunities both for learning as an academic discipline and technical training of direct help to industry. It has numbered among its presidents and lecturers many of the nation's most distinguished scientists, writers, composers and thinkers, including Charles Dickens, Anthony Trollope, Charles Kingsley and T.H. Huxley.

Dickens in Birmingham

Dickens gave some of his earliest public readings to raise funds for the Institute and became its President just before he died. He knew Birmingham well and in *Pickwick Papers* gives a most vivid description of the town as it was just before the coming of the railways:

It was quite dark when Mr. Pickwick roused himself sufficiently to look out of the window. The straggling cottages by the road-side, the dingy hue of every object visible, the murky atmosphere, the paths of cinders and brick-dust, the deep-red glow of furnace fires in the dis-

142

47. A Birmingham school of today. There are almost 200,000 children being taught at over 500 schools in the city.

tance, the volume of dense smoke issuing heavily from high toppling chimneys, blackening and obscuring everything around the glare of distant lights, the ponderous wagons which toiled along the road, laden with clashing rods of irons, or piled with heavy goods — all betokened their rapid approach to the great working town of Birmingham.

As they rattled through the narrow thoroughfares leading to the heart of the turmoil, the sights and sounds of earnest occupation struck more forcibly on the senses. The streets were thronged with working people. The hum of labour resounded from every house, lights gleamed from the long casement windows in the attic stories, and the whirl of wheels and noise of machinery shook the trembling walls. The fires, whose lurid sullen light had been visible for miles, blazed fiercely up in the great works and factories of the town. The din of hammers, the rushing of steam and the dead heavy clanking of engines, was the harsh music which arose from every quarter.

Not quite twenty years after the birth of the Institute came the foundation of a Science College. It was endowed by Sir Josiah Mason, who made a fortune from his pen factory, and with it provided a large orphanage for poor children at Erdington. These orphans were given preference of admission to this new college.

Science College for city

143

The Science College, in Edmund Street, included in its curriculum scientific teaching for medical students. This happened for a rather curious reason. A serious decline in the standard of medical teaching befell a unit known as Queen's College. A churchman benefactor, the Rev. Dr Warneford, became too influential and succeeded in persuading the anatomist Dr Sands Cox, founder and head of Queen's College, to add theology, law and engineering to his syllabus. Consequently, the college was reported to have fallen under the control of theologians at the expense of medical men. It was because of this unhappy situation that Josiah Mason College provided scientific training for medical students. This is the reason why, when the Science College was eventually converted into a university, the medical school remained an integral part of the university.

The University of Birmingham

Transformation of the college into a university was a major achievement. Nobody campaigned harder than Joseph Chamberlain and J.T. Bunce, Editor of the *Birmingham Post*. They raised the necessary funds locally and encouraged Birmingham businessmen to set their sights higher than a university college within a loose Midland Federation of Colleges — their objective was a Royal Charter for a full university.

In 1900 the University of Birmingham, at Edgbaston, became the first university in England since the founding of Oxford and Cambridge to be designed for a single city.[3] The University of Birmingham quickly expanded to meet the needs of an influx of students and developed its own 'persona'. The Nonconformist founders stipulated that it should be free from religious observances and vigorous in promoting the academic study of disciplines relevant to industry and commerce.

Science and engineering — and such unexpected subjects as industrial fermentation, which is closely allied to the brewing of beer — have given this university a very individual identity and local colour.

Support from Japan

The Faculty of Commerce, one of the first business schools in the country, was started at the request of Joseph Chamberlain. It attracted so many students from the Far East that in

144

1920 the Japanese firm of Mitsui endowed a Chair of Economics in the university. At the time there was more enthusiasm from Japan than from English firms and students, too many of whom have long continued to undervalue the importance of specialist training for industry and commerce.

Today the University embraces as wide a range of faculties as any other important university and spreads over a large part of Edgbaston. Happily, the splendid old trees and green open spaces of this garden suburb have not only been saved but also used with taste and imagination to provide the basic landscape of the interesting and beautiful new university campus.

Birmingham was also to the fore in establishing fine botanical gardens. Although Kew Gardens in London – presented to the nation by Queen Victoria in 1840 – were the greatest of these nineteenth-century institutions, the Botanical Gardens in Edgbaston were opened in 1830 and have ever since been a rich source both of horticultural knowledge and pleasure to students, townspeople and visitors alike.

The Botanical Gardens

Soon after the Botanical and Horticultural Society was formed the 12-acre site was acquired at Holly Bank, Edgbaston, and later extended to 16 acres. Advice on design and planting of the gardens was given by John Loudon, one of England's three most illustrious nineteenth-century gardeners (not counting famous landscape designers). Apart from such features as the arboretum, ferneries and roses, a magnificent elliptical conservatory became one of the finest examples of hothouse plant cultivation in the country.

Against the inherited Puritan background, which was somewhat dour and killjoy, a number of enlightened businessmen took steps to encourage a greater taste for culture in Birmingham. The most influential of these was Samuel Timmins – a Shakespearian scholar of international repute and by trade a maker of steel toys. Timmins gave many books to the Birmingham Library. These form the basis of what has now become a world-famous Shakespeare Library (it has published a seven-volume catalogue of the 40,000 volumes it contains). The only other comparable collection of Shakespeariana in the world is America's Fogler Shakespeare Library, in Washington.

A Shakespeare Library

The first Free Library was opened in Birmingham in 1861 and 'so great was the excitement' — we are told in the first annual report — 'that for several weeks applicants had to wait upwards of an hour before their turn to be attended to'. Four years later the Central Free Library was opened and work proceeded on the collection of books for a Reference Library,[4] the opening of which followed in 1866.

At the opening of the Reference Library fine paintings were exhibited. (These pictures, the gift of local citizens, were later transferred to a public Art Gallery which was opened in the Central Library building in 1867.) An inaugural speech was given by Mr George Dawson (see also Chapter 14), a speech which has been described as one of the most eloquent efforts of 'the first of English talkers'. Here is part of it:

> There are few places I would rather haunt after my death than this room . . . I wish that in the years to come, when we are in some aspects forgotten, still now and then in this room the curious questions may be asked: who gathered these books together? who was the first man that held the new office of librarian? I trust his name will be printed whenever the name of this Corporation appears . . . I am glad the Corporation has given itself an officer who represents intellect — that it looks upward deliberately and says 'we have made provision for our people, for *all* our people, and we have made a provision of God's greatest and best gifts unto man.'

History of newspapers

The story of Birmingham's newspapers is one both of failures and a few great successes. For the two years between 1741 and 1743 there was rivalry between a new *Gazette*, founded by Thomas Aris, a printer from London, and a more amateur-ish effort started a short while before by a Mr Walker and referred to simply as *Walker's Journal*. This journal was incor-porated with its more professional rival in July 1743 and the title was changed to *Aris's Birmingham Gazette*. This title in 1862 became part of the *Birmingham Gazette and Des-patch Ltd* until that company was absorbed by the *Birming-ham Post and Mail Ltd* in 1956. Of the historic Aris journal a complete file of all copies was preserved — one of the very few such files of an eighteenth-century newspaper in this country.

48. The opening of the Birmingham Central Free Library in 1865. The Reference
Library opened the next year but was tragically burned down in 1879. Only one
thousand of its fifty thousand volumes was saved. The latest Central Library,
opened in 1974, houses over a million books.

Today we regard 'controlled circulation' newspapers (i.e.
paid for by advertising revenue and distributed free) as a
modern publishing phenomenon imported from America,
but as long ago as 1836 just such a free newspaper was
launched in Birmingham, called the *Midland Counties Herald*.
There is scant evidence as to what happened to this free
sheet, but by 1838 it seems to have been eclipsed by a
weekly publication called *The Birmingham Journal*, claiming
a circulation of around 3,500 copies.

Newspaper reading was increasing in the taverns and coffee-
houses and, although it was illegal, newspapers were hired out
to groups of people in the town — this at a time when an
inquiry in 1839 showed that only one in every eleven people
in Britain could read. Often a workshop would buy a paper
as a group and one person would read it to the others. In
Birmingham public readings were started in the Bull Ring,

147

Union Street and other areas. There was no lack of new publications, but most of them failed to last long. They included the *Birmingham Magazine*, a literary and scientific journal edited by the Rev. Hugh Hutton, which first appeared in November 1827 and ran for only nine issues; the *Birmingham Daily Press*, launched on 7 May 1855 and which lasted two years; and the *Daily Globe*, a Conservative halfpenny evening newspaper which ceased publication eleven months after it first appeared on the streets on 17 November 1879. Yet another short-lived publication was a newspaper printed in German and launched on 7 August 1866.

The outstanding newspaper success story in Birmingham is that of the *Birmingham Daily Post*. One of Britain's leading provincial newspapers, the *Post* (it has a sister newspaper, the *Evening Mail*) was first issued on 4 December 1857. It has, by enterprise, a succession of distinguished editors and first-rate management, continued ever since as a powerful influence not only in the life and industry of our Second City but in the nation's affairs generally.

Notes

1. When the Elementary Education Act was passed in 1870 only half of Birmingham's 60,000 children attended school. It was not until 1890 that the law forbade children under eleven to work in factories.

2. Finally, when Joseph Chamberlain was the Minister responsible for education, he provided a compromise solution which gave a local authority the right to select its own governing boards to control the administration of their local Board schools. In 1902 School Boards were abolished by an Act which gave local authorities full powers of administration over education of all types up to university level.

3. In 1966 there followed the University of Aston, formerly a College of Advanced Technology.

4. A copy of William Caxton's 1479 masterpiece 'Cordiale' — worth £50,000 and one of only fourteen surviving copies produced by Caxton, the first English printer — has recently been bought by Birmingham Public Libraries. The city Librarian, Mr Brian Baumfield, described the purchase as 'quite simply the result of civic pride'.

17. The Arts-and Leisure

Many sophisticated people in Britain seem to suffer from a strange ignorance of Midland cities such as Derby, Sheffield or Nottingham and, perhaps, particularly Birmingham. There is a belief that the Midlands are ugly, grimy, uncouth and philistine. It may surprise such people to know that Birmingham never lacked an élite of cultured men and women prepared to give time, energy and money to fostering intellectual and artistic interests.

The pursuit of culture

For very many years Birmingham has enjoyed the benefits of a famous library, a municipal museum and art gallery, a symphony orchestra of international fame and a well known repertory theatre. The City Museum and Art Gallery is situated in the Council House. 'Big Brum', the clock which is Birmingham's equivalent of Big Ben, stands above it. These large galleries house a diversity of exhibits which include painting and sculpture by past and present great European and British masters, natural history, a philatelic collection, silver, porcelain, dress and, last but not least, the remarkable Pinto collection of domestic woodwork utensils. The gallery is particularly famous for its large collection of drawings and paintings by the pre-Raphaelites. The pre-Raphaelite brotherhood, a Victorian group of English painters, worked in clear, vivid colours with extraordinary attention to detail and many literary connotations. Their influence was felt in France at the birth of Impressionism, then lapsed until recent years when, in spite of their heavy sentimentality, they have found favour with the *avant-garde*.

The municipal Art Gallery and Museum opened in 1885. Its main acquisitions were donated by Thomas Osler, who both

A fund to buy pictures

made a collection and initiated a fund, now known as the Public Picture Gallery Fund. This has provided many important new acquisitions.

It was Thomas Osler's glass factory that was responsible for the grand centerpiece of the Great Exhibition of 1851 in the Crystal Palace which caused such a major stir in its day. The idea for the Great Exhibition, which aimed to promote trade and improve standards of design and manfacture, was born of a visit by Prince Albert to a Birmingham Trade Fair. The Crystal Palace building was put up in a great rush and against fierce opposition from local inhabitants. However, in spite of the doom-watchers, it was ready to open on time, very largely due to the efficient way Birmingham produced both the huge and vital iron girders and the vast quantity of sheet glass.

The Barber
Institute

Of equal standing as a picture gallery, but much smaller than the City Art Gallery, is the Barber Institute of Fine Art at the University of Birmingham, Edgbaston. Sir Henry Barber, a lifelong governor of the University (he practised for a while as a barrister in Birmingham), inherited wealth from the family firm of Bird's (custard). Sir Henry's widow formed a trust at his request to provide and endow an institute for the fine arts generally, for the advancement of music and musical education, and for the further development of the Faculty of Law.

So it was that the Barber Institute came into being, opened by Queen Mary in 1939. Here, in addition to the galleries which are open to the public, is a fine concert hall which offers free concerts for members of the University, a music school, and a department of fine art with an excellent library.

Dr Thomas Bodkin, an engaging Irishman (he was reluctant to let outsiders visit the gallery and kept it closed as much as possible!) had the enviable task of buying pictures and *objets d'art* for the collection. By the time he retired Dr Bodkin had put together an excellent small collection (mostly European art up to the end of the nineteenth century) and the gallery is now thought to be one of the best small galleries in Europe.

A Birmingham Society of Arts was founded in 1809 to provide art education and exhibitions of the work of contemporary painters — including one of our first water-colour artists David Cox, who lived locally. Queen Victoria honoured the Society by conferring the title Royal. It has since been popularly known as the RBSA and owns an exhibition gallery in New Street.

Like the Crystal Palace, the quick development of the Midlands Arts Centre for Young People, in Cannon Hill Park, was a revolutionary concept. It was dreamt up by the playwright John English and his wife Alicia Randle. Despite the belief of many local big-wigs that the dream would never become a reality in bricks and mortar, the project went ahead. The first building, Foyle House, opened as an administrative centre, art gallery and small concert room in 1964. It is now a hive of creative activity for young people within the wide age span of 5 to 25 years. The Centre is open seven days a week, from early morning until late at night, averaging more than a thousand 'session attendances' a day. At weekends and in holiday times facilities are available for family groups.

This outstanding arts centre aims to promote education in, and appreciation of, the arts amongst young people. It offers a comprehensive programme of films, concerts, theatre performances and puppet shows as well as an extensive range of sports and arts facilities for members of its club, Midland schools and other groups. John and Alicia English devoted themselves totally to the Midlands Arts Centre for Young People and can now look back with pride on their creation. It is a truly remarkable pioneering project, particularly at a time of general financial difficulties.

The achievement was, in part, made possible by the formation of the Cannon Hill Trust which raised money from private individuals and from corporate bodies. Contributions to the Trust have been matched by central and local government finance. The Centre quickly acquired a high reputation, both at home and abroad, and this has led to a large number of enquiries and visitors to Cannon Hill Park anxious to see the enterprise for themselves.

'Almost all the big towns of England manifest some leading

151

taste or other', wrote Hugh Miller[1] over a century ago. He considered that of Birmingham to be a taste for music, induced as a restful contrast to living where there was

> an increasing clang of metal, an unceasing clank of engines ... where flame rustles, water hisses, steam roars ... where even the imprisoned linnet or thrush is excited to emulation by the knife-grinder's wheel, or the ding of a coppersmith's shop, and pours out its soul in music.

Musical development in the city began with the first Birmingham Festival, held in 1768 in aid of the General Hospital. Handel's music was performed by an orchestra of 25 players and a chorus of 40 singers. The Birmingham Festivals were subsequently held at irregular intervals before becoming biennial events.

By the middle of the nineteenth century the Birmingham Festival was able to move into the elegant new Town Hall and so gained much in dignity and importance. In 1837 the great Mendelssohn conducted his St Paul, and appeared as organist; nine years later he and his friend, Ignaz Moscheles, the Bohemian pianist and composer, shared the conducting in Birmingham of the first performance of Elijah. Both the St Paul and Elijah oratorios were composed especially for the Birmingham Festival.

It was also in Birmingham that Antonin Dvořák, another great Bohemian composer (destined to follow his father as an innkeeper and butcher) conducted the first performance of his 'The Spectre's Bride' and his Requiem Mass — the latter at the Birmingham Festival of 1891.

During the First World War Birmingham subsidised an orchestra from the rates, and in 1920 the Birmingham City Orchestra was founded with the help of a guarantee from the municipality. The City Orchestra later became the now internationally known City of Birmingham Symphony Orchestra and among its early conductors was Sir Adrian Boult — subsequently conductor of the BBC Symphony Orchestra.

England's first rep. theatre

The country's first and most famous repertory theatre, derived from an amateur band of actors known as the Pilgrim

152

Players, was established in Birmingham in 1913 by Barry Vincent Jackson, son of a wealthy Birmingham merchant. Sponsoring the theatre from his private fortune, Barry Jackson ran it until his death in 1961. Affectionately known simply as 'the Birmingham Rep.', this was a training ground for many actors and actresses who later became famous and many hundreds of plays, old and new, were produced here.

The Alexandra Theatre is, in part, also a repertory theatre, but provides for companies on tour as well. It traditionally puts on a long winter season of exceptionally high-class pantomime which draws family parties by the bus-load from far and near.

The first theatrical entertainments for the people of Birmingham were provided in the seventeenth century by companies of strolling players giving shows in fields where Temple Street now stands. These players performed 'drolleries' (jesting acts) from some of Shakespeare's plays. By 1743 there was a theatre in New Street and the *Gazette* carried an announcement of a production of *Morning Bride*, by the renowned Yorkshire-born dramatist William Congreve. Four years later another theatre opened in Moor Street with a tragedy called *The Siege of Damascus* which, said an announcement, would have 'proper dresses to every character and scenes and decorations proper to the play'.

Early in the nineteenth century the Theatre Royal opened and among many illustrious actors to appear there was Edmund Kean, famed for playing tragic roles. Three times the Theatre Royal in Birmingham was destroyed by fire.

Throughout the nineteenth century the popular level of entertainment was catered for by music-hall, which soon outgrew the concert rooms in the larger public houses. Music-hall flourished in Birmingham and drew large audiences up to the coming of the cinema in the first years of the twentieth century. By 1914 there were 53 cinemas in the city.

Music-hall entertainment

The idea often put forward that the entire canal-side of the city could become like the fashionable Vauxhall or Ranelagh pleasure gardens of Victorian London is nowhere better expressed than in Birmingham's new Repertory Theatre, now

Canal-side developments

49. The 'Home of the Iron Convenience' was a nickname given 19th century Birmingham on account of its ornate ironwork street lavatories. The picture below shows a typical small back-street Birmingham public house, complete with 'iron convenience'.

situated in Broad Street near the canal basin. It is a modest but elegant building, liked by both actors and audience, and has a café and bar open to the public as well as theatre-goers, the idea being that if you go in for a beer, you may buy a theatre ticket! It is to Birmingham's credit that this enterprising project is yet another step towards making the city centre the 'united' place it always was — and not, as modern planning all too often means, dividing life into artificial compartments of work, refreshment, culture and the family.

There have recently been other imaginative improvements along the canal-side, but there is still more to be done if the city is to make full use of what has been termed a 'leisure gold-mine'. The 1969 bicentenary celebrations of the Birmingham Canal Navigations attracted attention to the debt the city owes its canals and the splendid opportunities that exist for a new leisure-time use of these waterways and their pathways — hidden and ignored for too many years. Flatteringly, Holland (with 3,000 miles of navigable canals and rivers) recently sent a delegation to study how this country is solving the problems of disused canals — of which we have 1,700 miles as against only 300 miles carrying freight.

In the field of sport Birmingham has long been a centre for professional and amateur football, cricket, lawn tennis and boxing. The city can boast over one hundred years of first-class football and is widely known for its successful Birmingham City Football Club, founded in 1875, Aston Villa, founded one year earlier, and West Bromwich Albion; in cricket Edgbaston is a classic ground; and in tennis the championships held by the Warwickshire Lawn Tennis Association are events of the highest order. (It was in 1864 that a Major Gem and a Mr Perera were playing a game on the lawn of a house called 'Fairlight' in Ampton Road, Edgbaston — their new game became known to the world as lawn tennis.[2])

A hundred years of football

For a hundred years the city has been one of Britain's major brewing centres. The two big breweries are Ansells at Aston Cross, and Mitchells and Butlers at Cape Hill. Ansells was founded by the Birmingham maltster and hop merchant Joseph Ansell, who started brewing beer with his sons at Aston in 1830. The business grew rapidly, so that by 1901, when this brewery started bottling beer, Ansells was worth

A name in brewing

50. There is over 100 years of football history in the city. Here are the 1887 Football Association cup winners, Aston Villa.

over £750,000. Just as the engineering firms were doing in Birmingham, Ansells next bought smaller breweries and ultimately merged itself with other large firms to form a group called Allied Breweries Ltd.

The history of the rival Birmingham brewery M & B began in 1866 when two Midland men, Henry Mitchell and William Butler, began brewing beer at Smethwick. As their business expanded, Mitchell found a new site at Cape Hill whilst Butler was becoming famous for his home brew at the Crown Inn, in Broad Street. These men formed the M & B firm in 1898.

Davenport's is the third Birmingham brewery with a long history. In 1829 Robert Davenport was a brewer at Hockley and it was his grandson John who first made beer available in bottles for people to drink at home. To this day the Davenport business thrives mainly on its 'beer at home' policy.

156

Birmingham has every kind of inn and public house, ancient
and modern. The City Information Section even has its own
well illustrated leaflet as a visitor's guide to the city's best in
beers and pub food.[3] Among the historic pubs are the beautiful Old Crown, in High Street, Deritend, partly rebuilt in
1830 but fortunately largely as originally designed by Robert
O'Greene in 1368. Another is the Crown, in Broad Street
next door to the first M & B brewery; in the bars are the
nineteenth-century Matthew Popham paintings of distinguished Birmingham citizens, including Sir Thomas Martineau,
Alderman Thomas Avery and Sir John Ratcliffe.

At Aston, the splendid Bartons Arms is preserved in all its
Victorian glory but now stands in isolation in a depressing
redevelopment area. The pub contains much stained glass,
heavy mahogany woodwork and thousands of patterned tiles
on the walls. A large stained glass window lights the main
staircase and the bar partitions have shutters (they used to be
called 'snob lights') which allowed people to see into the bars
while remaining hidden in the hall. This magnificent monu-
ment to Victorianism was built in 1901. Variety stars and
such famous stage personalities as Chaplin and Caruso used to

51. Stained glass at
the Bartons Arms,
Aston Newtown.

stay at Bartons Arms when appearing at nearby Aston Hippodrome.

A few miles to the north of the city centre on the way to Sutton Coldfield is Warwickshire's oldest pub — The Lad in the Lane, at Erdington, dating from 1306. During the Civil War, Roundheads and Cavaliers used this inn on occasion and local tales have it that a secret tunnel led from the Inn to Aston Hall (see picture, p. 37).

In the 1930s and again after the last war there was a boom in new pubs of a grandiose kind, catering for wider social purposes than the old-fashioned pub. A number of these were built in and around Birmingham, including The Swan at Yardley — acknowledged in the *Guinness Book of Records* to be Britain's largest pub, having banqueting and conference rooms as well as a restaurant noted for its French cuisine. The pub can accommodate over 1,000 people at a time. An earlier example of the battle for pub 'respectability' on the grand scale was The Antelope, a building in impeccable taste put up in the Stratford Road in 1922. The architect was Holland W. Hobbis, and the sculptured doorway was designed by William Bloye, a pupil of Eric Gill, sculptor and typographer. There are many other impressive new pubs in the Birmingham area; nowhere was the vogue for larger and grander licensed houses pursued more vigorously than here. Fortunately this development was not carried out at the expense of colourful and historic inns, the determined preservation of which is a feature of Birmingham.

Notes

1. Hugh Miller, *First Impressions of England and Its People*.
2. Dorothy McCulla, *Victorian and Edwardian Birmingham from Photographs* (Batsford, 1973).
3. Another excellent source of information is *Birmingham Pubs 1890-1939* (Centre for Urban and Regional Studies, University of Birmingham, 1975, in association with the Victoria Society, Birmingham Group).

18. A New Industrial Era

In the last years of the nineteenth century Great Britain lost her lead in the Industrial Revolution — although Birmingham remained one of the economic capitals of the world. Not only had Britain used up much of the easily won supplies of iron-ore and coal, but her industry was less readily adaptable to the new era of cheap steel and electricity than were the industries of the USA, Germany and France.[1] America and Germany challenged Birmingham's industrial supremacy with better management, new factories equipped with modern machines and by making not only the same sort of articles but selling them more cheaply.

Challenge from overseas

To counter the financially depressing effects of overseas competition — particularly on the iron and steel industries — Birmingham, under Chamberlain's leadership, organised a petition to Parliament which resulted in the Tariff campaign of 1903. Tariff changes, plus the fact that Birmingham workers were not slow to adapt their skills to new trades — an important one being the making of bicycles — brought a marked recovery in trade both in Birmingham itself and the surrounding Black Country.

New methods were the vogue and entrepreneurs took advantage of Birmingham skills to set up large, well organised firms in the city. Many of these businessmen came from the Continent, where they had benefited from scientific training of a kind not then available in England. Among the scientists from Germany was Ludwig Mond.[2] The Mond family introduced modern nickel production techniques and later Mond's chemical works[3] at Winnington Hall, Cheshire, provided the main foundation of Imperial Chemical Industries.

52. & 53. 19th-century Birmingham was the source of the best glass obtainable anywhere in the land. Thomas Osler, renowned as 'glass chandelier furniture manufacturers' of Birmingham, designed this splendid fountain for the 1851 Great Exhibition at the Crystal Palace (left). Birmingham also supplied and erected in record short time the iron girders for the Crystal Palace (picture shows trusses being raised in the centre aisle). With the help of the London and North Western Railway, iron from the foundry of Fox & Henderson was in position at the Crystal Palace often within eighteen hours of leaving Birmingham.

The new industrialists acquired patents from the USA for a number of mass-production machines. An example of this was a machine for carding (i.e. separating) pins, and hooks and eyes. At the 1851 Great Exhibition at the Crystal Palace the Nettlefold firm in Birmingham bought a USA patent for mass production of wood screws — these are the familiar metal screws with a pointed end which screw directly into wood.

Birmingham held her position as the prime producer of finished metal goods from about 1830 onwards. Although many of the traditional small workshops in the heart of the city carried on, there was a considerable merging of firms resulting in large combines — Stewart and Lloyd, steel producers, being but one example, today's Guest, Keen and Nettlefold (GKN) being another. Agents and commercial travellers began making direct contact with British customers at home and abroad.

Empire trade benefits

Birmingham kept in close touch with all the colonies of the British Empire, providing them with large quantities of

160

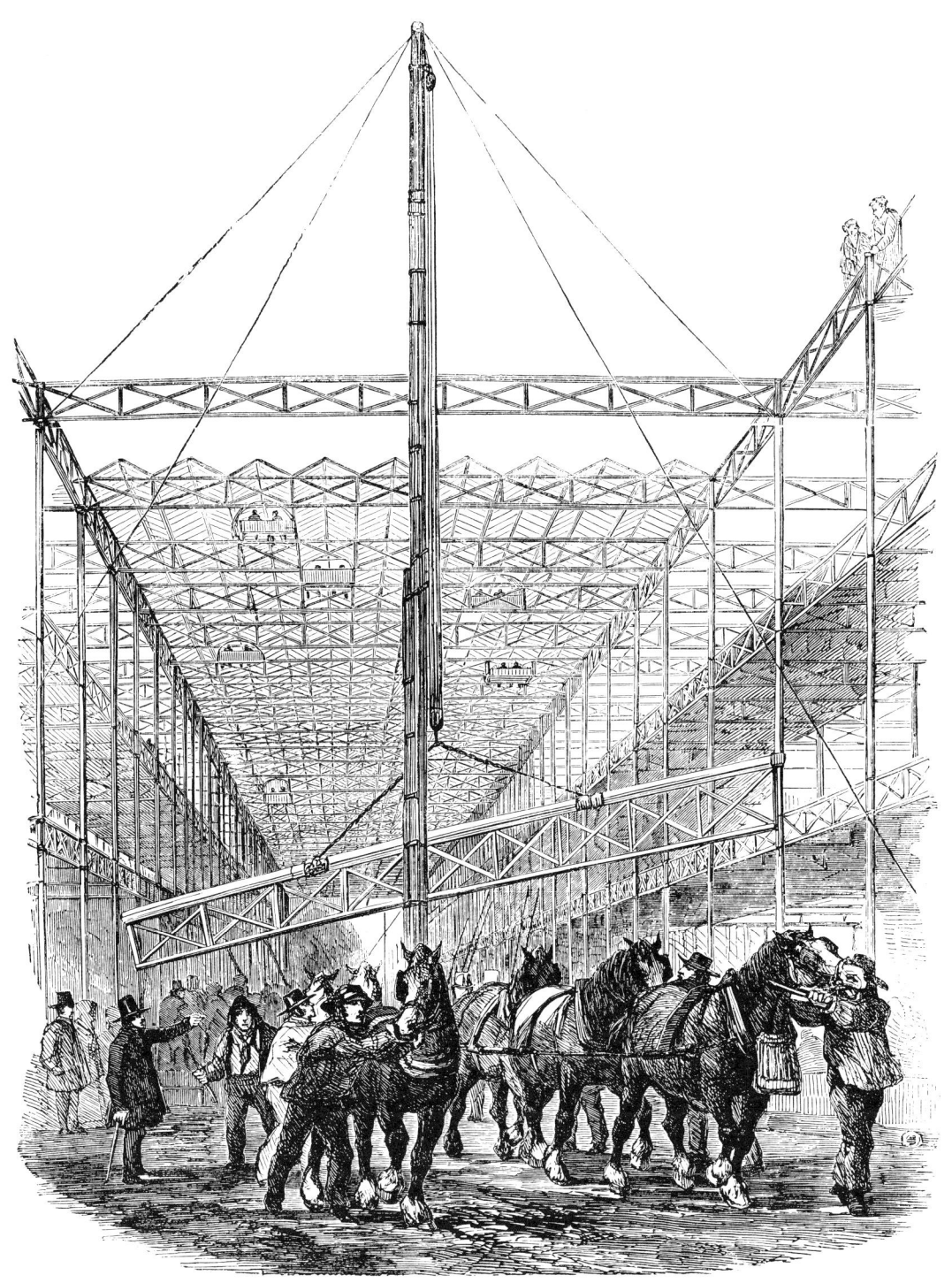

engineering equipment and sending out engineers to advise on the installation and maintenance of Birmingham-made machinery. A valuable side-effect of this trade with the Empire was the availability of new materials from overseas, including latex from Malayan rubber trees — and this led to the development of the tyre industry at Fort Dunlop, Erdington.[4] The import of cocoa from Africa was another example, leading to the expansion of the world-renowned Cadbury firm in Birmingham.

The boom in cycling

This was also the time when big engineering works were being built in the suburbs outside the city centre, following the earlier example of Cadbury's chocolate factory at Bournville and the Birmingham Small Arms Company at Small Heath. BSA, as the company was generally called, was among the early concerns to take advantage of the boom in cycling (a useful sideline to the making of guns). The cycling vogue, both as a sport and for practical transport, came in with the Coventry invention of the 'safety' bicycle in 1885, superseding the 'ordinary' or 'penny-farthing' design and being propelled by a chain to the rear wheel instead of direct front-wheel pedals.

Everywhere young men and women took up cycling so that the 'safety' bicycle became a popular way of getting to work in the factories. The brass- and tube-makers in particular took to making cycles and before the First World War ten thousand people worked in the Birmingham cycle trade. Besides a vast output of cycle tyres from Fort Dunlop, other Birmingham firms made cycle equipment, including saddles and lamps. Joseph Lucas, a lamp-maker in the city, brought out his special 'King of the Road' cycle lamp and it sold in its thousands — laying the foundations for the giant Lucas firm, one of the largest in Birmingham and now internationally known for all types of electrical equipment in transport.

Recently, in this age of the motor car, there has been a keen revival of interest in cycling both as a sport and as a practical and healthy means of transport. With an output — mostly from the Midlands — of over a million cycles a year (more than half are exported) cycle-making is one of the country's most successful international industries.

162

54. After 'Engineer Extraordinary' Isambard Kingdom Brunel failed five times to launch his iron ship the *Great Eastern* for the purpose of laying the first Atlantic telegraph cable the Birmingham firm of Tangye Brothers brought him success (in 1858) with hydraulic lifts. Among the tense faces watching launching efforts are Lord Derby (extreme right) and next to him Brunel.

It was in Birmingham that the first Atlantic telegraph cable was made for laying across the ocean by an iron ship — the *Great Eastern*. The launching of this vessel proved very difficult; its designer Isambard Kingdom Brunel, famed for his railway and ocean steam navigation work, tried five times without success to launch the monster ship. It was the biggest challenge to Brunel's distinguished career and he finally succeeded in 1858 when he called in the Tangye Brothers, a Birmingham firm of machine-tool makers, who provided hydraulic lifts to get the *Great Eastern* into the water. In 1869

Laying the Atlantic cable

163

this ship helped lay some of the first telegraph cable across the Atlantic and the up-and-coming Tangye company in Birmingham was able to boast 'we launched the Great Eastern and she launched us!' But Brunel lived only long enough to see his iron ship afloat. He died in 1859, before any of the ship's great voyages.

Electricity takes over

From the first years of this century electricity started to take over from steam and gas. Electricity soon became the new and transforming source of power. In 1901 the General Electric Company (known far and wide simply by its initials GEC) opened at Witton, a Birmingham suburb. By 1911 seven thousand people earned their living from electrical work in and around the city — most of this work being connected with the cycle and fast-growing car industries.

As the trend away from the city centre to factory sites in the suburbs (where land was cheaper) increased, so did the residential areas around the factories. To serve these districts the city council encouraged the provision of horse-drawn buses, steam trams and a suburban train service. Then, in 1904, the Corporation took over from the private operators and established a Birmingham Transport Department; two years later electric trams replaced the steam trams. The horse, alas, was on its way to almost total disappearance from the streets of Birmingham — even the great Horse Fair, which had been a much-loved feature of Holloway Circus, ceased in 1911.

The start of Austin cars

It was outside the city centre, at Longbridge five miles away, that Herbert Austin in 1905 bought a two-acre site for a car factory and the first Austin car left the Longbridge works the following year. By 1914 the output was 1,500 cars a year. Today the Austin factory is the size of a small town, with 27,000 workers.

The Austin company's first merger was with Morris Motors of Oxford, to become the British Motor Corporation (BMC for short). Next, in 1968, BMC joined forces with Leyland Motors to form British Leyland. Very recently another change took place whereby the car production of the group is known as BL Cars and the commercial vehicles revert back to the name of Leyland.

164

About the same time that Herbert Austin started at Longbridge a Birmingham engineer, James Norton, made the first of a long line of classic motor-cycles. Norton machines became the world's leading racing motor-cycles. At Small Heath the BSA company were making motor-cycles in ever-increasing quantities and these were soon to be found in every part of the world.

The First World War gave a big boost to most Birmingham manufacturers. The basic metal industries such as machine tools, motor vehicles, cycles and the staple trades of brass-founding[5] and jewellery all prospered.

Wartime boost for trade

Like all Birmingham factories during the war, the BSA company concentrated on munitions. From a little over one hundred rifles a week before 1914 this firm was now producing 10,000 rifles every week, apart from much else needed by the services. So, too, at Lucas. There, many thousands of women were busy making shell covers, dynamos and aeroplane parts. At Longbridge all types of war transport were being turned out by the Austin concern: they even had their own railway station built to bring in the workers who travelled by train. In the chemical industries it was the same story of expansion and volume output. Only some small, newly established trades in Birmingham went down in the First World War, never to resurface.

The Armistice of 1918 found Birmingham on the crest of a wave of prosperity. This carried the city over the first few years of peace. After that, however, Birmingham gradually became caught up in the national economic depression which reached its full impact in the early 1930s. Almost all trades suffered. Yet, despite the slump civic progress was continued. Municipal housing became the most urgent need in this city as elsewhere, largely due to the cessation of housebuilding during the war.

Many of the earliest municipal housing estates were built far from the city centre, with the result that the middle classes moved away from central Birmingham, leaving behind them only the poorest sections of the population. This shift to new residential districts a few miles out had a number of repercussions on social life, not the least being a decline in the function and status of the churches and chapels. Suburban housing also eventually eroded much of the distinctive quality of Birmingham politics.

Notes

1. Up-to-date geological surveys now reveal the East Midlands to have the biggest untapped reserves of coal in Western Europe.

2. Great-grandfather of Lady Zuckerman.

3. Mond metal, a new alloy, was one of several new alloys introduced into the Birmingham brass trade in the early 1920s. A few years later the Mond Nickel group, ICI Metal Divisions and Henry Wiggin & Co. combined to provide other new alloys.

4. Rubber manufacture of all kinds started in Birmingham as early as 1862, the most important maker being Dunlop.

5. 'Brass has been to Birmingham what cotton has been to Manchester' — Professor Asa Briggs, Professor of History at the University of Sussex.

19. The Modern City

Of industrial England, Sir John Betjeman has written:

> Do not judge industrial towns by their faces; they are
> the most alive places in England; they are more interes-
> ting than the little dead country towns which we so
> like to look at: think of Manchester and Birmingham
> with their concerts, theatres, parks, art galleries . . . to
> someone who likes people as well as buildings, the
> industrial towns are the hope and life of England.

Birmingham, the city of Matthew Boulton and James Watt,
which made so great an impact at the beginning of the
Industrial Revolution, is today a regional capital and among
Europe's most up-to-date cities. Its new National Exhibition
Centre (see next chapter) is a focal point for trade and
industry on an international scale. The West Midland region,
of which the city is now part, is an industrial and engineering
conurbation matching in size the German Ruhr.

A regional
capital

In its modern image Birmingham began to flourish after the
Second World War. Industrially, enormous developments in
the electrical industry had become well established in the
city. Giant generators were built for the world's power
stations as well as a large range of electric motors, switch-
gear and electrical furnaces. The food industries also grew
rapidly, partly because — as happened after the First World
War for a time — there was full employment and an adequate
variety of foods. Women continued to work after the war and
local wages were higher than the national average.

During the war Birmingham suffered heavily. Over two thousand of its citizens were killed and another six thousand

167

injured in 77 German air raids.[1] Factories, workshops, offices and many hundreds of homes were destroyed. But this devastation gave the old Birmingham of small, congested workshops and great clusters of slum homes its Phoenix-like opportunity to arise from the ashes with renewed vigour, whilst at the same time retaining its proud heritage of invention, industry and trade. It is even claimed[2] that in the bombing of Birmingham 'rather less was destroyed than the city council might, after reflection, have hoped.' But what Hitler failed to do, the partnership of developers and councillors has accomplished very effectively.

A £200 million building task

The city's first redevelopment officer, Neville Borg, was appointed in 1952. The scheme for slum clearance and redevelopment of the city under post-war planning legislation was the first attempt of its kind, on a large scale, in Britain. It was a £200,000,000 task, equivalent to the building of several new towns. In just two years between 1966 and 1968 Birmingham built more new houses than Liverpool, Manchester and Sheffield put together (incidentally, the first building society to help people buy their own homes was formed by Richard Ketley in 1775, at the Golden Crown Inn in the city). Today, Birmingham is the largest housing authority in the land.

All this vast activity in housing, plus the city centre reconstruction, greatly influenced transport services within the West Midland conurbation. By 1956 Sir Herbert Manzoni — Neville Borg's predecessor as City Engineer[3] — had already drawn up plans for a new network of motorways based on a 'cartwheel' design around a central hub, its 'spokes' running out to the boundaries of the city.

Air connections between Birmingham and other parts of the world have been increasing ever since the city created its own airport at Elmdon in 1939. Latest developments include weekday flights to Copenhagen and a much-increased service to Brussels, the European Economic Community capital. Railway electrification, station modernisation and new road traffic arrangements have wrought great physical change on the centre of the city. New Street Station has been completely rebuilt and Snow Hill (another classic station of early railway days) closed down. Inter-City electric trains now run

168

55. & 56. Nothing could show a greater contrast in the city centre than these gabled little dwellings in Queen's Head Yard about 1875 (soon afterwards demolished in the Steelhouse Lane Improvement Scheme) and today's nearby Bull Ring Shopping Centre. The sign in the yard of the Queen's Head was a painting of a Penny Black stamp of Victoria's reign.

half-hourly between London and Birmingham and the journey takes only ninety minutes.

These enormous changes in traffic flow and communications generally cause the pedestrian in modern Birmingham to have a rather exhausting time! It is a blessing, of course, that he is unlikely to be run over, but to ensure his safety he has to walk up and down many stairways and, like a rabbit, find the right hole to emerge from among the warren of corridors underground. The feeble, or even the active but weary walker, can take comfort from the wall decorations intended to keep up his spirits as he reminds himself that he is underneath the nation's most important transport communications centre. If he makes it to the very heart of the system, emerging at the Bull Ring shopping precinct, he can claim his reward by mounting the moving staircase to the peace and quiet of traffic-free shops, or the extensive market which supplies fresh foods to the whole industrial area for miles around, or to the bus station, restaurant or car park (all enveloped under one enormous roof). Architecturally, the concept is not as distinguished as it should be, but is certainly highly practical.

Changes in car industry

For most of the 1950s and 1960s the West Midlands and prosperity were synonymous, but times have changed. During this decade the car industry, a vital part of the region's economy, has suffered increasing problems caused by labour disputes and much fierce overseas competition. Plants making car components, aluminium alloys, iron castings and hand tools have also been affected by trade recession. Those companies which have remained profitable have largely done so by determined expansion of exports.

Today Birmingham has over half its total work-force in manufacturing industry. The big combines such as Leyland, GKN, Lucas, Tube Investments, Dunlop, Cadbury-Schweppes, Delta Metal, Albright and Wilson, and IMI form the heart of the Birmingham economy. Increasingly, Birmingham industry is not only linking up with that of the United Kingdom as a whole, but also with its counterparts abroad. For instance, the GKN firm has purchased a German components company as part of its drive to capture a larger share of the European market. Another example is the Dunlop Rubber Company, which, half a century ago, had not much more than four

170

thousand people making tyres for cars and cycles now employs over 100,000 people — half of them outside the UK — making a very large range of products from tyres to tennis balls, from pipelines to pillows. Dunlop now sells in one hundred and fifty territories around the world.

Names not perhaps thought of in connection with an engineering city have, however, long been prominent in Birmingham's industrial progress. Best known is, perhaps, that of Cadbury and its internationally admired model factory complex at Bournville. The firm was started in the mid-nineteenth century and the Cadbury family have been leaders in civic and philanthropic work ever since (see also Chapter 12).

Chocolate and toys

Also known the world over is the Chad Valley Company, makers of table games and children's toys since the beginning of the century. The forerunner of the present company (named after the Chad, a small river running beside the works at Harborne) was a printing and bookbinding firm set up in Lichfield Street in the city by Anthony Johnson. This

57. Inside a Birmingham factory about 1905 — making children's toys at the Chad Valley Company, 'Toymakers to the Queen' by Royal appointment.

business started in the 1820s and in 1897 moved out to Harborne, trading as Johnson Brothers. It amalgamated with two or three small toy manufacturers and, as Chad Valley Ltd, grew very rapidly.

Many children's games of the time still retained the educational aspect that had been their origin. Jig-saw puzzles were an aid to learning history, geography and other pictorial subjects; even the familiar Snakes and Ladders game was designed to point to virtues and morals. Soft toys were later added to Chad Valley's imaginative range of games. Factory extensions became necessary and by 1932 the six-storey works had become a landmark over a wide area of south-west Birmingham.

Progress was marked by the granting in 1938 of the Royal Warrant of Appointment — 'Toymakers to Her Majesty the

58. In 1840 a local historian recorded that 'we have not to chronicle any more the brutal and demoralising sports in the history of the amusements of the people' . . . particularly 'lewd fellows of the baser sort'. In place of bull-baiting with dogs 'gentlemen were friendly to the project of providing ground for the encouragement of cricket, racket and other games'.

Queen'. The year 1950 saw the end of Chad Valley as a private family business when it was made a public company. Now recognised as the brand leader in the UK soft-toy industry, in 1978 the company once more changed ownership. It was bought for £1 million cash by the largest toy manufacturers in the world — General Mills of America.

As elsewhere in the United Kingdom, immigration has become part of the civic scene in Birmingham although, in fact, Indians and Pakistanis arrived in the city long before immigration control became a political issue. When, later on, the West Indians and Africans first arrived, not only did they add a further pleasant touch of colour to the streets, but they were peacefully absorbed into the life-style of the city. In making this possible part of the credit has to go to organisations such as the Sparkhill Association, which led the way in helping to create new kinds of community relationships. Politics and attitudes applied in Birmingham, in many fields besides the integration of coloured people, have frequently given a lead to others.

It is deep in the Birmingham character to be ready to try something new. One example in the field of social service was the first hospital devoted exclusively to accident cases, Birmingham Accident Hospital, which now also houses the world's most up-to-date unit for the treatment of severe burns. The city continues to pioneer enterprises which are attracting attention not only throughout the United Kingdom but also overseas.

Notes

1. Lord Zuckerman directed the Ministry of Home Security survey of Birmingham casualties.
2. Anthony Sutcliffe and Roger Smith, *Birmingham 1939-45* (*History of Birmingham*, Vol. 3) (Oxford University Press, 1974).
3. Birmingham's No. 1 appointment is that of City Engineer; elsewhere it is City Architect.

59. An aerial view of
the National Exhibition
Centre showing the
landscaping of the site
with trees, shrubs and
a man-made lake
stocked with over ten
thousand fish.

20. The Exhibition Centre

The National Exhibition Centre — opened by the Queen in February 1976 — provides certain proof of Birmingham's leadership and modern enterprise. This £39 million purpose-built venue for international exhibitions and conferences has a continuous floor space of 90,000 square metres — at least twice the space at Olympia in London and all at ground level. It is comparable in size with the Crystal Palace, constructed in London's Hyde Park for the 1851 Great Exhibition.

Proof of leadership

Conservationists approve the landscaping since fewer than ten established trees were felled by the builders and the surrounding natural woodland has been extended by the introduction of 60,000 more trees and shrubs, together with a man-made lake stocked with 10,000 fish. With the opening of this Exhibition Centre a dream of thirty years became a reality. It was a project which fired the imagination of Midlanders. To have succeeded despite opposition from London, and even considerable hostility, has undoubtedly boosted Birmingham's confidence.

The Centre, an exhibition township in itself complete with luxury hotel, is a unique example of what can be achieved when local businessmen and politicians find a common cause — in this case the improvement of Britain's vital export trade. A share of the credit for this achievement goes to Robert Booth, Director of Birmingham Chamber of Commerce in 1968 when a House of Commons Select Committee on Export Promotion toured Britain, inviting views on the siting and development of a national exhibition centre.

Improving export trade

Mr Booth — now Sir Robert Booth, Chairman of the National

Exhibition Centre Ltd – was supported by Mr Frank Cole, President of the Birmingham Chamber of Commerce and a director of companies operating road, rail and air freight. But it was finally the determination of Sir Francis Griffin, leader of the Conservative-controlled Birmingham City Council, supported by his Labour colleague Sir Frank Price, that won the day for Birmingham by offering to take responsibility for financing the Exhibition Centre.

Within hours of the news reaching Birmingham, in January 1970, that the then Labour government – impressed with Birmingham's case – had given approval to the project, city officials went to Bickenhill (seven miles out towards Coventry) and bought the 310-acre site for a quarter of a million pounds. Four months later NEC Ltd was formed with eight directors, equally divided between the City Council and the Chamber of Commerce.

Today the Exhibition Centre is attracting 80 per cent of the major industrial exhibitions in Britain. The Centre is host to the industrial world, its communications unrivalled. Birmingham Airport lies alongside; Birmingham International is a new railway station specially built to serve the exhibition halls and linked to them by covered walks and escalators. This is the first entirely new station to be built in Britain since 1899. For road travellers a pattern of specially built roads provides access from surrounding motorways.

More cash for
the Midlands

In its first year the National Exhibition Centre brought an estimated £25 million spending money into the Midlands and provided nearly 3,000 much-needed full- or part-time jobs. Boosted by the Centre (its big events include the Motor Show and a number of important exhibitions previously held only in Continental cities) Birmingham is now rapidly gaining status as a leading banking as well as exhibition city, with national and international banks moving new branches to Birmingham.[1] An insurance company has announced plans to build on a city centre corner site a seven-storey new office block – 'the finest in the city'.

Moving with
the times

These are changing times and Birmingham is moving with them. The city's population is now a great mixture of people from many countries. There are Irish, West Indians and

176

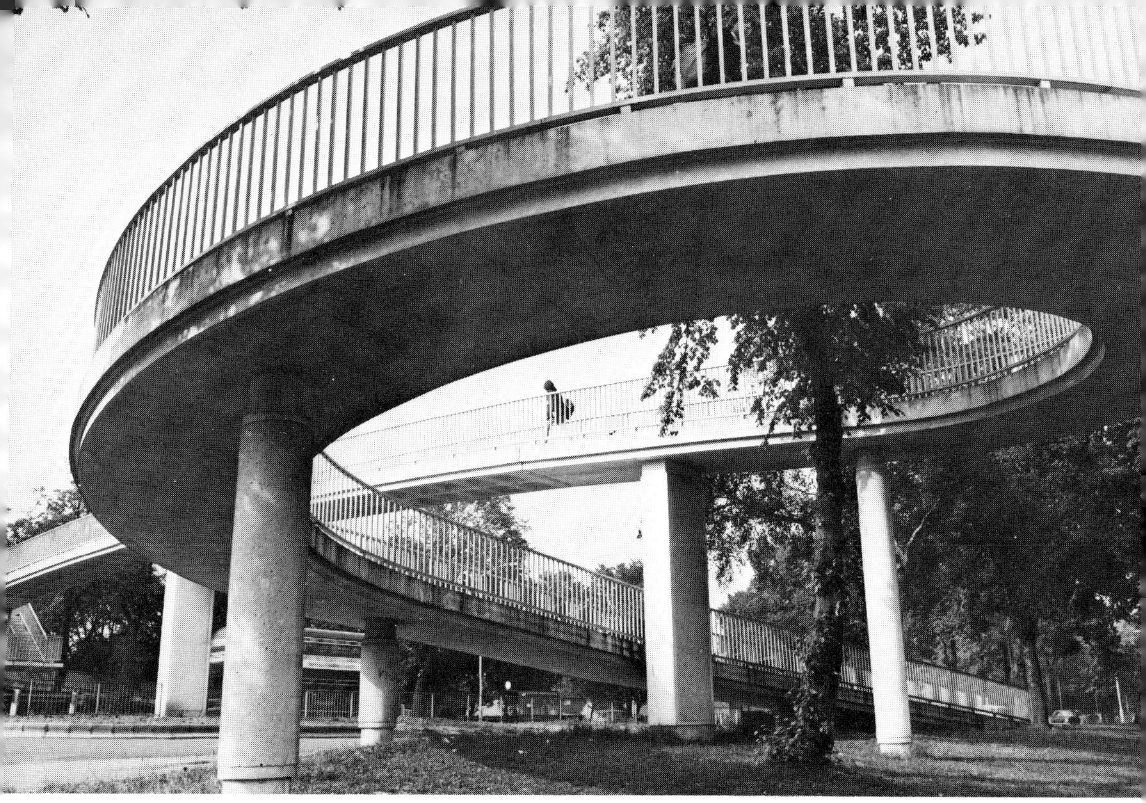

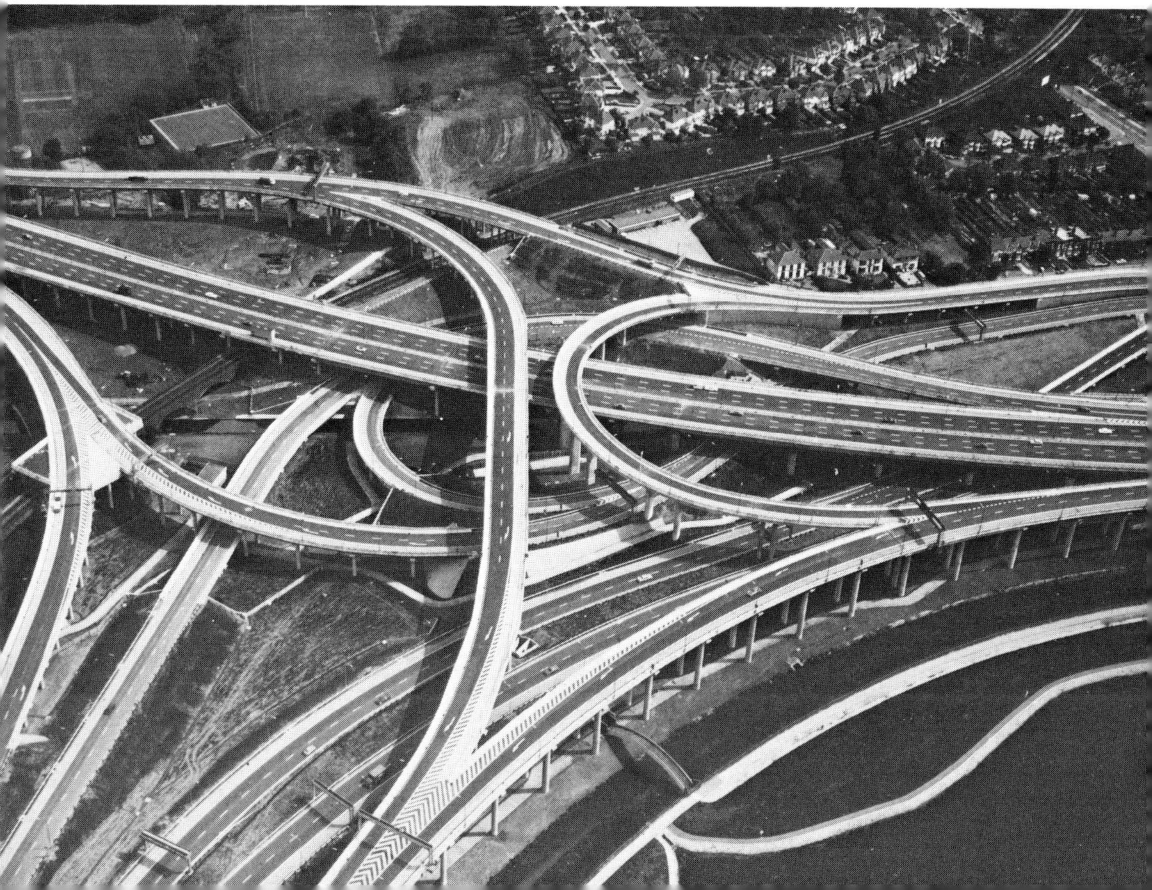

Asians working and living in the city. Of course, when jobs are scarce, and with housing always in short supply, difficulties are bound to arise. However, the particular qualities of Brummagems — and it is on these qualities that the city has built its great reputation — are based on skills and hard work, with the drive and flexibility of mind to adapt to change and to move forward with the times.

Modern Birmingham is a pivot in Britain's bid to be a competitive member of the European Economic Community. Its industrial and cultural links overseas are further fostered by the 'twinning' of Birmingham with four European cities — Frankfurt, Lyons, Milan and Zagreb — and with the Russian metal and chemical centre of Zaporozh'ye.

Surely, England's Second City will never cease to play a major part in Great Britain's future. *'Forward'*, the motto Birmingham chose for its coat of arms so long ago, remains true of the spirit of this distinguished city today and to-morrow.

Note

1. Birmingham has long had a unique Municipal Bank and its own Stock Exchange.

Appendices

APPENDIX 1: TOURIST INFORMATION CENTRES

City of Birmingham Publicity Section, 110 Colmore Row,
    Birmingham B3 3SH (Tel. 021-235-2051)
National Exhibition Centre, Birmingham B40 1NT
    (Tel. 021-780-4141)

APPENDIX 2: LIBRARIES, MUSEUMS, ART GALLERIES
AND HISTORIC HOUSES

Central Lending and Children's Libraries; Music Library;
Visual Aids Department, Reference Library (8 subject depart-
ments)
Opening hours: Monday and Friday 0900–1800; Tuesday,
    Wednesday, Thursday 0900–2000; Saturday 0900–1700
Birmingham and Midland Institute, Margaret Street, Birming-
    ham (Tel. 021-236-3591)
Museum and Art Gallery, Chamberlain Square, Birmingham
    (Tel. 021-235-2834)
Museum of Science and Industry, Newhall Street, Birming-
    ham (Tel. 021-236-1022)
Barber Institute of Fine Arts, The University, Edgbaston,
    Birmingham (Tel. 021-472-0962)
Birmingham Nature Centre, Cannon Hill Park, Pershore
    Road, Birmingham (closed Tuesday except following Bank
    Holidays) (Tel. 021-472-7775)
Birmingham Railway Museum, Warwick Road, Tyseley,
    Birmingham (Tel. 021-458-3934, evenings only)

Aston Hall, Trinity Road, Aston. Built 1618-35
Sarehole Mill, Hall Green. First mill, sixteenth century
Weoley Castle, Alwold Road, Selly Oak. Late thirteenth
    century

Blakesley Hall, Yardley. 1550-1600.
(The above four are Branch Museums of Birmingham City Council.)

Selly Manor and Minworth Greaves, Handsworth. Thirteenth and fourteenth century (run by Bournville Village Trust)
Botanical Gardens, Westbourne Road, Edgbaston

APPENDIX 3: SOME INTERESTING CHURCHES

St Philip's Cathedral, an outstanding example of classic Baroque style built in 1715 to the design of Thomas Archer of Warwickshire. It contains magnificent stained glass windows by Sir Edward Burne-Jones, born in Birmingham and christened in this cathedral.

St Martin's in the Bull Ring has, throughout the centuries, been Birmingham's 'church in the market place'. It is the city's parish church and was rebuilt in 1873 — although there has been a church on the site since 1085. It has some fine monuments to the de Bermingham family, local lords from whom the city derives its name.

St Chad's in Bath Street was the first Roman Catholic Cathedral to be built in England after the Reformation. Completed in 1841, it is the work of the celebrated Houses of Parliament architect Augustus Welby Northmore Pugin.

St Paul's, in St Paul's Square, used to be known as 'the jewellers' church'. In the second half of the nineteenth century its parish housed many of the city's jewellers and craftsmen. Earlier, the scientific pioneers Matthew Boulton and James Watt had pews there.

The Methodist Central Hall in Corporation Street, built in the 1900s, is noted for its fine Italianesque campanile and its staircase.

The Roman Catholic Oratory of St Philip Neri, on the Hagley Road, is an ornate building in the Italian Renaissance style. It is a place of pilgrimage for Catholics from many lands.

At Bournville is the remarkable *Serbian Orthodox Church of*

St Lazar. Built in 1965-8 in the fourteenth-century Serbian Byzantine tradition, it is the only modern church of its kind in Europe outside Yugoslavia. It was designed by the Belgrade architect Dr Tadic, and the interior was fashioned entirely by Serbian craftsmen. Worshippers regularly attend from many parts of the UK.

St Mary's, Handsworth, contains memorials by Charles Flaxman to Matthew Boulton, James Watt and William Murdoch.

Holy Trinity, Sutton Coldfield, has many relics of historical value and a vault in which lie the remains of Bishop Vesey of Exeter, founder of the sixteenth-century grammar school.

APPENDIX 4: FACTORIES AND COMPANIES OPEN TO VISITORS
(Note: Adequate notice of a desired visit should be given.)

A.P.E. BELLISS
Icknield Square, B16 0QL (Tel. 021-454-3531)
Trade: Air compressors and ore crushers
Days & Times: Tuesday to Thursday
Apply to: Personnel Department
Maximum Party: 20
Notice Required: At least 14 days
Schools: Yes

BIRMINGHAM CO-OPERATIVE SOCIETY
High Street, B4 7SP (Tel. 021-643-5071)
Trade: Milk processing, laundry
Days & Times (a) Dairy, Vauxhall Road, B7 4HL (Monday to Friday 10.30 a.m. — 2.00 p.m.)
(b) Laundry, Holyhead Road, B21 OAD   ) Wednesday
(c) Bakery, Manor Road, Stechford   ) at 2.30 p.m.
Apply to: Personnel Services Controller, High Street, B4 7SP
Maximum Party: 20 in each case
Notice Required: Seven days
Schools: Yes — Central premises including offices, Monday—Friday

BIRMINGHAM POST & MAIL
Colmore Circus, B4 6AY (Tel. 021-236-3366)
Trade: Newspapers
Days & Times: Weekday afternoons 2.00 p.m.
　　Saturday 10.00 a.m.
Maximum Party: 12
Notice Required: As much as possible
Schools: Yes (over 12)

BRITISH ELECTRICAL REPAIRS
Church Road, B42 2LE (Tel. 021-356-5021)
Trade: Electrical & mechanical engineers
Days & Times: Any day except Saturday by arrangement
Apply to: Works Manager
Maximum Party: 10
Notice Required: By arrangement
Schools: Yes (over 14)

CINCINNATI MILACRON
Kingsbury Road, B24 OQU (Tel. 021-351-3821)
Trade: Machine tools
Days & Times: Monday – Friday 2.00 p.m. – 4.00 p.m.
Apply to: Manager, Engineering (for general visitors);
　　Training Manager (for students and trainees)
Maximum Party: 8-10 restricted to engineers and associated
　　trades
Notice Required: 7 days. Less if unavoidable for overseas
　　visitors
Schools: Only senior technical and commercial students

THOMAS HADDON & STOKES
Deritend, B12 OLW (Tel. 021-772-2312)
Trade: Screws, bolts, nuts & washers
Days & Times: Monday to Friday
Apply to: Personnel Manager
Maximum Party: 10 (larger parties by arrangement)
Notice Required: As much as possible
Schools: Yes (over 15)

ARTHUR HOLDEN & SONS
Bordesley Green Road, B9 4TQ (Tel. 021-772-2761)
Trade: Varnishes, enamels & lacquers
Days & Times: Afternoons except Saturday

Maximum Party: 12 technical visitors only
Notice Required: 14 days minimum
Schools: Sixth-formers only

IMPERIAL METAL INDUSTRIES (KYNOCH)
Kynoch Works, Witton, B6 7BA (Tel. 021-356-4848)
Trade: Copper, titanium, zirconium, hafnium, niobium and
   tantalum, metal components for all industries; sporting
   ammunition
Days & Times: By appointment
Apply to: Recruitment Officer
Maximum Party: 20
Notice Required: As much as possible
Schools: Yes (over 15)

MIDLAND ELECTRIC MANUFACTURING
Reddings Lane, B11 3EZ (Tel. 021-706-3300)
Trade: Electrical switch-gear, Motor Control Gear, Accessories
Days & Times: By arrangement
Apply to: Training Supervisor
Maximum Party: 20
Notice Required: 8 weeks
Schools: Sixth-formers

ANSELLS
Aston Brewery, Aston Cross, Birmingham
   (Tel. 021-327-4747)
Trade: Brewers
Days & Times: 3 days weekly, by arrangement
Apply to: Commercial Department
Maximum Party: 30
Notice Required: By prior arrangement
Schools: (over 14)

TUBES LTD
Rocky Lane, B6 5RH (Tel. 021-359-3030)
Trade: Seamless steel tubes and manipulated forgings
Days & Times: Monday to Thursday afternoons
Apply to: Training Officer
Maximum Party: 15
Notice Required: One month
Schools: (over 14)

TUFNOL LTD
P.O. Box 376, Perry Barr, B42 2TB (Tel. 021-356-4562)
Trade: Industrial Plastics
Days & Times: Tuesday and Wednesday afternoons
Apply to: Training Officer
Maximum Party: 6
Notice Required: 3 months. Preference to students and
    technical visitors
Schools: Yes

WICKMAN SCRIVENER TAYLOR & CHALLEN
Brookville Road, Witton, B6 7EX (Tel. 021-356-6881/8)
Trade: Grinding machines, lathes, presses, coining machines
Days & Times: Tuesday, Wednesday and Thursday afternoons
Apply to: Sales Manager
Maximum Party: 10
Notice Required: Three weeks. Visitors should be technically
    or commercially interested
Schools: Yes (over 15)

Select Bibliography

Bird, Vivian. *Portrait of Birmingham*. Hale, 1970

Birmingham Before 1800. Maps and colour prints. Birmingham Public Libraries

Birmingham Information Department. *Portrait of Birmingham* (first published 1969)

Birmingham Pubs 1890-1939. Centre for Urban and Regional Studies, University of Birmingham, 1975, in association with the Victoria Society, Birmingham Group

Briggs, Asa. *Victorian Cities*. Penguin Books, 1968

British Association for the Advancement of Science (1950). *Birmingham and its Regional Setting*. Reprinted by EP Publishing, 1970

Broadbridge, S.R. *The Birmingham Canal Navigations*. David and Charles, 1974

Clark, Kenneth. *The Gothic Revival*. Murray, 1962

Court, W.H.B. *Rise of the Midland Industries — 1600-1838*. Oxford University Press, 1938

Defoe, Daniel. *A Tour Through the Whole Island of Britain*. Penguin English Library, 1971

Delieb, Erich, and Roberts, Michael. *The Great Silver Manufactory — Matthew Boulton and the Birmingham Silversmiths 1760-1790*. Studio Vista, 1971

Dent, Robert K. *Old and New Birmingham* (originally published 1878). Reprinted in three volumes by EP Publishing, 1972

Dorman, C.C. *Birmingham Railway Scene*. Town and Country Press, 1971

Dorman, C.C. *The London and North Western Railway*. Priory Press, 1975

Hartwell, Ronald Max. *The Industrial Revolution and Economic Growth*. Methuen, 1971

Hill, Christopher. *Reformation to Industrial Revolution*. Weidenfeld & Nicolson, 1967

Hoskins, W.G. *The Making of the English Landscape*. Hodder and Stoughton, 1955

Hutton, William. *History of Birmingham* (first published 1782). Reprinted by EP Publishing, 1969

Judd, Dennis. *Radical Joe.* Hamish Hamilton, 1977

King-Hele, Desmond. *Erasmus Darwin.* Macmillan, 1963

Kitson Clark, G. *The Making of Victorian England.* Methuen, 1965

Little, Brian. *Birmingham Buildings.* David and Charles, 1971

McCulla, Dorothy. *Victorian and Edwardian Birmingham from Photographs.* Batsford, 1973

Millward, Roy, and Robinson, Adrian. *Landscapes of Britain — West Midlands.* Macmillan, 1971

Newbold, E.B. *Warwickshire History Makers.* EP Publishing, 1975

Pardoe, F.E. *John Baskerville of Birmingham.* Muller, 1975

Pevsner, Nickolaus, and Wedgwood, Alendra. *Warwickshire.* Penguin, 1966

Powell, Enoch. *Joseph Chamberlain.* Thames & Hudson, 1977

Prosser, R.B. *Birmingham Inventors and Inventions* (originally published in 1881 as a limited private edition). Reprinted by EP Publishing 1970

Robbins, Michael. *The Railway Age.* Routledge & Kegan Paul, 1962

Rolt, L.T.C. *Narrow Boat.* Eyre and Spottiswoode, 1944

Rowlands, Marie B. *History of Industry in Birmingham.* City of Birmingham Education Department, 1977

Schofield, R.E. *The Lunar Society of Birmingham.* Oxford University Press, 1963

Schoyen, A.R. *The Chartist Challenge.* Heinemann, 1958

Showell, Walter. *Dictionary of Birmingham* (first published at Corn Wells Brewery, Oldbury, in 1885). Reprinted by EP Publishing, 1969

Stanton, Phoebe B. *Pugin.* Thames and Hudson, 1971

Sutcliffe, Anthony, and Smith, Roger. *History of Birmingham,* vol. 3. Oxford University Press, 1974

Tann, William. *Midlanders Who Made History.* Wayland, 1973

The Birmingham Post 1857-1957. Published by the Birmingham Post and Mail Ltd

The Great Exhibition of 1851 — A Commemorative Album. Victoria and Albert Museum, 1964

Victoria County History — Warwickshire. Dawson and Sons.

Whybrow, J. *How Does Your Birmingham Grow?* Whybrow, 1972

Index